NO REFLECTION, ARE YOU WHO YOU THOUGHT YOU WERE?

No Reflection, Are You Who You Thought You Were?

Christopher Johnson

Copyright © 2016 by Christopher Johnson
All rights reserved. No part of this book may be reproduced in any manner whatsoever without written permission except in the case of brief quotations embodied in critical articles and reviews.
First Printing, 2016

Introduction

Note: wherever satan is not capitalized is my purpose. I refuse to give him that privilege regardless of the grammar rules.

I, Chris Johnson, a believer in God the Father, Jesus (*The Risen Savior*), God's only begotten son, and the Holy Spirit of God that comforts and guides us to the things of God, have encountered many people who need to tell me things about their lives, some I know and some I don't; people like to share things with me. A stranger would share personal things, and when asked why I was the choice to tell, they would answer: "It is just something about you." "You are a good listener." I listen not to respond, but to hear what they are saying because they want to be heard. David Harris is the one who encouraged me to write this book; we would have "round table" discussions about the things they told me. David is also a guest writer in this book.

These writings come from a collection of quotes spoken frequently by those who chose to tell me about their lives, whether or not the true meaning is known by those who speak them, they sound interesting, so people use them. I acknowledge those I know, but there are some for whom the author is unknown. These are things you may have already read or heard, but not as they are written here; the authors may have intended a different meaning, but God has shown me how to arrange them in a collective manner that would bring awareness to what we thought we knew and who we thought we were. I believe, that even though some of these quotes come from non-believers, God still used them for His good because God is always; He often speaks to open ears and open hearts, but not necessarily to everyone who hears, but those that are receptive to His word. (*'metal and aluminum shavings look alike, making it hard to tell the difference, one from another, but when a magnet is used only the metal shavings will be dis-*

turbed by the magnet, then you will know which is which"-Unknown); those that struggle to understand the meaning of His words, he provides a tutor. These writings are comprised mostly of "round table" discussions David and I had every week. If we change how we process information, we will change the way we live. Everyone who reads this book will not agree that the truth will always be the truth, even when not seen as such. I believe awareness is the key to the truth, and these writings are presented to promote awareness of what and who we thought we were.

Man sees himself in his children, and that is a joy, but when he sees that part of himself he dislikes in his children, he despises that part, yet, he changeth not. I hope that all who see themselves in these writings will change the way they look at others and acknowledge that they are not much different from those they pass judgment on and that we need each other to survive. Hopefully, we can realize that God is the final judge.

Overview

(David Harris & Chris Johnson)

It is not often that we don't see ourselves in the mirror at some point or another. The point varies, but mostly involves a detailed inspection of our outward appearance, which is always exposed to the world. We go to great lengths to ensure what people see is the best outward appearance we can offer, yet we work less on what's on the inside. That includes the mental, physical, and spiritual aspects of who we are.

People spend a great deal of time and money on things that make them look like someone other than themselves (*i.e., plastic surgery, wrinkle removers, hair they were not born with, etc.*), but are cheap when it comes to spending time and money to look like themselves. What I mean is: that some will spend more money on an outfit that makes them appear to be something they are not, to please people that are strangers that they may never see again, but will not invest in their relations with those they see daily; learning who they are, that you might seek their greatest good, helping them to see you as one who cares for them.

These internal factors have more weight than anything else in determining who we are, how we think, and, most importantly, how we act. We tend to pay more attention to others' behavior as we freely pass judgment on how we think they should act, yet we don't look back at our actions and do the same.

We seem to be far less critical of our actions for some reason, which is no big surprise, as it's very easy to rationalize our actions to justify what we want to do. It seems as though right and wrong have taken a back seat to wants and wishes that we have, regardless of the negative consequences that may result from our decisions. We find ourselves in a time where blaming our mistakes on someone else is considered the new normal, and responsibility is valued only when a positive outcome is desired or achieved. If anything negative results from our actions or decisions, we automatically default to deflecting responsibility somewhere, but not where it belongs, with the one who made the decision. We have to ask ourselves: how much of our current situation are we responsible for? How did we get to this point in our lives where we believe that what we are doing is okay? "Deception"

How often do we reflect on the decisions we make? Better yet, how often do we research a subject and gather information before making a decision? When was the last time you questioned what you believed to be true to verify the information you have been given? Do you consider or dismiss opposing points of view? Do you welcome a debate of issues, or limit yourself to those who share your ideology and beliefs? Do you seek knowledge and desire to know the truth, or do you accept what is comfortable and convenient for you? The fact is, most of us fail to recognize that what constitutes our idea of a said truth may not be the truth at all. These are questions we should pose to ourselves before we ask them of others, and there's no better place to start than the next time you find yourself standing in front of a mirror.

Self-evaluation (*Metacognition*) must be encouraged if we hope to reach a higher level of understanding about what we do and why we do it. We have to be honest with ourselves when evaluating our true motivations, which lead directly to our actions. If we are not honest with ourselves, what does that say about us? Does it concern you? Does it bother you? And if not, ask yourself why? It's a natural fact: we are all born selfish and self-centered. A newborn's only instinct is selfishness, as it has a need and desire for warmth, food, and protection, as it can provide nothing for itself. We know nothing else at this stage but desire, and the more we are given, the more we want, which, if gone unchecked, is a recipe for narcissism on a grand scale. Hopefully, we are taught by our parents and teachers to be unselfish as we grow older. The search for understanding is not just a journey, but also a battle. A battle waged within each of us to fight the instinct to serve ourselves above all others, as we must all learn to be unselfish, *David Harris & Chris Johnson.*

"Every man must decide whether he will walk in the light of creative altruism or in the darkness of destructive selfishness," *Martin Luther King, Jr.*

Preface

"And be not conformed to this world: but be ye transformed by the renewing of your mind, that ye may prove what is that good, and acceptable, and perfect, will of God" *Romans 12:2 KJV*. "The person without the Spirit does not accept the things that come from the Spirit of God but considers them foolishness, and cannot understand them because they are discerned only through the Spirit"(*1 Corinthians 2:14 NIV*). Those who believe must pray, asking God to remove their blindness, so that they might see what the good and acceptable will of God is. These writings are to bring awareness of what is true. If "*they*" don't believe the truth, does that change the Truth? It seems as though "*they*" have considerable power over our thinking. The popular phrase" *they* say this is the best, etc."Are you who "*they*" say you are? Are you who you thought you were? Consider who "*they*" are. Well, this "*they*" has been identified as the world (*The majority*). John 4:5 *NIV* "They are from the world and therefore speak from the viewpoint of the world, and the world listens to them".

Contrary to popular belief, the majority is not always right; in the story of Noah and the Ark, you will see that the majority was wrong. The majority (*the world*) says: live like this, and you are successful; live like this, and you are not. Remember, success might not be to them what it is to you. After all, it was "*they*" who crucified Jesus. GOD said: obey my word, and you shall have the desires of your heart within his will. Most prefer what *they* say because we have been enslaved by "*they*"; we do what "*they*" say without challenging the outcome, but when God tells us what we must do, we challenge His instructions to see if it's right for us. The wise will hear and increase their learning, and the person of understanding will acquire wise counsel *and* the skill [to steer his course wisely and lead others to the truth], To understand a proverb and a figure [of speech] *or* an enigma with its interpretation, And the words of the wise and their riddles [that require reflection]", *Proverbs 1:5-6 AMP*". Someone once said that "freedom has a corresponding slavery; whatever you want to become good at, you become a slave to" (*cause and effect*). Here, it seems as if most want to become good at what "*they*" say. What do "*they*" know? Did "*they*" make you? "The maker or creator of a thing knows its intended use. To obtain knowledge of a particular thing, one must consult the maker," M*iles Monroe*. Are you who you thought you were? *Proverbs 2:2-5* states that if we want to know what God says as much as we do about what "*they*" say, we can know. But nothing so valuable can be so easily obtained; if it were, it would be of no value. Wisdom must be sought after with a strong desire to receive it. If the majority believes something is true, does that make it true? No, truth is truth, even if "*they*" don't believe it. Truth is freeing your mind from man's finite wisdom; we are victims of this version of wisdom. Incline your ears to God's instructions. This book is designed to promote wealth; if you believe wealth is only about money, then stop reading now. The only thing we have and need is worth more than anything else that can be valued. That is love, for God and one another. "Beloved, let us love one another, for love is from God, and whoever loves has been born of God and knows God". *1 John 4:7 KJV* "Love is when the other person's happiness is more important than your own." *H. Jackson Brown, Jr.*

Some will read this and remain the same because they think it doesn't apply to them. "Reason is not automatic; those who deny it cannot be conquered by it. Do not count on them; leave them alone", *Ayn Rand*. There will always be those who don't want to hear it, so don't force it, but instead, pray that God will remove their spiritual blindness. Be rich in love for all and be free of leaning to man's wisdom. "Love is patient and kind; love does not envy or boast; it is not arrogant or rude. It does not insist on its own way; it is not irritable or resentful; it does not rejoice at wrongdoing, but rejoices with the truth. Love bears all things, believes all things, hopes all things, endures all things. Love never ends. As for prophecies, they will pass away; as for tongues, they will cease; as for knowledge, it will pass away" *1Corinthian 13:4-8 KJV*. "The only thing necessary for the triumph of evil is for good men to do nothing", *Edmund Burke.* Pray that good men do something. "A friend is someone who knows all about you and still loves you", *Elbert Hubbard.* Pray for a friend like that.

"Being deeply loved by someone gives you strength, while loving someone deeply gives you courage", *Lao Tzu.* Pray for love like that.

"I have decided to stick with love. Hate is too great a burden to bear", M*artin Luther King, Jr.* Love means sharing our joys and our pains with the ones we love, and believing that the love between you and them is strong enough to withstand anything.

Table Of Contents

Chapter 1 Cause and Effect (*The end preexists in the means*)

Chapter 2 Going in Circles (*Round and Round I go*)

Chapter 3 Smarter than the Average Bear (*Yogi The Bear Syndrome*)

Chapter 4 It is what it is (*Perception is not always reality*)

Chapter 5 Self-inflicted wounds (*Whatever a man soweth that shall he also reap*)

Chapter 6 Dictated living (*Puppet Syndrome*)

Chapter 7 You didn't see because you were too busy looking (*The Vampire Syndrome*)

Chapter 8 Vanity (*I know this song is about me*)

Chapter 9 Greed (*not being content with what you have*)

Chapter 10 Deception (*O. what a tangled web we weave*)

Chapter 11 Hurry up and wait (*The Tortoise & the Hare*)

Chapter 12 Selfishness (*I'm just doing me*)

Chapter 13 Trust in God's Plan (*Without Faith it is impossible to please God*)

Chapter 14 Integrity (*Are you who you thought you were?*)

Chapter 15 Giving (*Have I helped someone today?*)

Chapter 16 Forgiveness (*How Soon We forget*)

Chapter 17 Being a Servant (*Do unto others*)

Chapter 18 Life's only true satisfaction (*What's Love got to do with it?*)

Chapter 1

Cause and effect
(*The end preexists in the means*)

"Cause and effect, means and ends, seed and fruit cannot be severed; for the effect already blooms in the cause, the end preexists in the means, the fruit in the seed", *Ralph Waldo Emerson*. Because of God, both exist, the fruit and the seed. Check out the way God did it: He put the seed in the fruit, but the fruit is also in the seed. *Genesis 1:29*

What we do affects more than just us. Our actions can affect many people, and our death affects the people we leave behind. If we oversleep because we stayed up late and left for our destination late, we find ourselves rushing the next morning; our mind is not focused on what we are doing, but on what we need to do. Herein lies the cause; it is our fault; we caused this situation, even if staying up late was due to circumstances beyond our control. We decided to leave in a rush; we decided to hurry; remember, we're already late. What's the rush? Now we are concentrating on what needs to be done, not what we are doing; carelessness sets in. Herein lies the effect: we now cause an accident on the freeway; hundreds of people are stuck in traffic. Our actions have affected others, causing them to suffer because we did not think of them before we acted in this way. "In each action, we must look beyond the action at our past, present, and future state, and at others whom it affects, and see the relations of all those things. And then we shall be very cautious", *Blaise Pascal, Pensées.*

There are so many ways our actions can affect others. Let's say we stay home from work, our job now has to suffer from our absence, and what we do at work; someone has to do our job and theirs (*Cause and effect*). What we must understand is that even when we go to our jobs and fail to do what we were hired to do, everybody suffers. If a mail clerk fails to do the job they were hired for, nobody gets mail on time; every piece delayed could be important enough for the CEO to make decisions concerning the company's business. We can cause so much harm to others by simple selfish acts; we should always consider the greater good before we act. "Through the law of cause and effect, we choose our destiny. Moreover, we are our own prophets for we constantly project our future state by the seeds we plant in the present", *Cheryl Canfield.*

Some states have an open container law, prohibiting drivers from having an open alcoholic beverage container in the vehicle. If you don't want to get caught with an open container, then don't open it in the vehicle; wait until you get home. When you drink it in the vehicle (*cause*), you are not thinking of properly disposing of the container when you finish (*effect*); you either throw it out the window or set it in the parking lot, either way, it becomes unsightly; empty containers on the side of the road or in a parking lot have no appeal. Now, when you get drunk and drive, of course, you don't think of anyone else because you are no longer in control. Truth: You have no concern or care for others, while drunkenness dictates what you do. Now, when you receive a certificate (*DWI*), don't forget that you earned it. *The end preexists in the means.* "Remember one thing about democracy. We can have anything we want, and at the same time, we always end up with exactly what we deserve", *Edward Albee.* The good thing, where God is concerned, we didn't get what we deserve because, through an act of kindness, God's grace was given. The cause: kindness; the effect: grace. Cause and effect, means and ends, *if you plant apple seeds, you will not grow peaches, only apples, that's just the way that works.*

Imagine this: you get drunk and say hurtful things to people you claim to love, or your drunkenness dictates that you cause them physical harm. Suppose you become addicted to a substance, be it cocaine, heroin, or whatever, and you steal from the one you say you love to support your habit. Maybe you committed adultery or fornication; either of these causes harm to the people you claim to love; to harm the loved ones is the same as not loving them at all. These are caused by your decision to allow these things to dictate your actions and affect your loved ones. Most have observed open packages in the stores, right? Well, this is called shrinkage; it is a lost sale; whether someone took none, all, or some of its contents; it becomes unsaleable because it has been opened. Who wants to purchase an open package? Not even the one who opened it. Some of you have witnessed a person (*most likely someone shopping with you*) open a package to feel or smell something; put it back and purchase the same product, but not the one they opened. When this happens too often, either the product gets locked up, and you have to get store personnel to unlock it, or the price goes up due to loss; either way, this act causes the effect to apply to all who seek this product. Those who commit these acts don't believe this to be true because they wear the blindfold of thoughtlessness.

It is easier to get people to believe a lie rather than the truth: The Santa Claus, the Easter Bunny, and the Tooth Fairy, etc.

If someone posted this on the internet: "By placing a live rabbit on the hood of your car, you will have good luck all day long and could become wealthy". The truth is, someone will believe it and try it. It will be believable only to those who always seek the unobtainable, and the unattainable rather than what is already at hand, e.g. a stack of money was secured with a rubber band; and placed at someone's feet, the wind started to blow the money around, and most would go after the floating money, but rather the money at their feet (*Greed*); that they may never catch. This is why the gospel is so hard to comprehend; the simplicity of it is hard to grasp for those who are too busy doing nothing (*chasing unobtainable and unattainable things*) while something (*investing time in what is at hand*) needs to be done (*"Why can't we just get in the running car?"*); those who desire to get paid (*want to go to heaven and receive a crown*) but are not willing to work (*follow the guidelines to receive what you seek*). Just like Wimpy on Popeye, "I will gladly pay you Tuesday, for a hamburger today." Deception is the cause; satan's lies that we choose to believe are the effect.

Deprivation (*cause*) allows one to know the significance of receiving something that helps them in many ways (*effect*). The one who has been deprived of warmth on a cold day will appreciate being warmed more than the one who has not been deprived. The one that has an abundance of warmth on a cold day tends to become too content. Well, the children of God tend to follow this trend too. When God blesses us too much, we become stale and unappreciative, some to the point of looking down on those who don't have what we have; it should be our desire that they enjoy what we enjoy. The blessings (*cause*) overflow, and without working out for God, we get lazy and don't want to do anything but receive (*effect*), you know what happens to people who eat too much and don't exercise. Could we, or would we endure what the Jews endured in *Nehemiah 8:3*, most likely not; church for two hours is too much for most; don't let the sermon last more than 10 minutes, the preacher gets all kinds of looks. Many examples can be given, but awareness is the key to the truth, and the truth will set your mind free. Fertilizers are used in lawns to aid and enhance growth. The Word of God is to a lost soul as fertilizer is to grass. A seed is planted, watered, and fertilized. *Cause*: Fertilizing grass (*lost souls*) with the word of God will strengthen their roots and help them grow strong. *Effect*: God will water as needed and draw them to Himself. We have to be the seed planters; God will create the harvest from that. Change will not occur nor be considered unless an alternative way of life is successfully introduced (also *what satan does through deception*). In other words, people would keep going in circles; when they met you, there was nothing there that drew them toward change; your light was dim. "Be the change that you wish to see in the world", *Mahatma Gandhi.*

If you are sick and tired of judgmental behavior, quit judging. If you are sick and tired of injustice, do not become one who practices or encourages it. If you are sick and tired of racism, don't practice any of the above, they are all forms of racism. "Behaviorism, also known as behavioral psychology, is a theory of learning based upon the idea that all behaviors are acquired through conditioning. Conditioning occurs through interaction with the environment. Behaviorists believe that our responses to environmental stimuli shape our behaviors. Strict behaviorists believe that any person could potentially be trained to perform any task, regardless of things like genetic background, personality traits, and internal thoughts (*within the limits of their physical capabilities*); all it takes is the right conditioning" *John B. Watson.* Racism is the opposite of these thoughts. *Cause:* you judge or practice injustice against another because you feel as though you are superior to them. *Effect*: Because of your action, someone now feels suppressed, angry, less than human, and so on. Does this honor God?

What is it about Christmas that causes people to get all giddy, happy, friendly, and giving? Some say: because of Christ's birthday; others say: 'Tis" the season to be jolly. Whatever! Could it be injustice because of your need to feel superior that has caused this, not Christ? This jolliness you feel, is guilt undercover? Is it the superior lifestyle you have lived all year that now you feel guilty and want to reach out to someone less fortunate? Yes, the effects are positive, but the motives are not pure. If it were because of Christ, you would feel this way all the time, not just at the end of the year; that's what love is. "Love is the cause that effectively affects people". "I refuse to accept the view that mankind is so tragically bound to the starless midnight of racism and war that the bright daybreak of peace and brotherhood can never become a reality... I believe that unarmed truth and unconditional love will have the final word", *Martin Luther King, Jr.*

A Washington apple is only that if it grows in Washington; a California peach is only that if it grows in California; Florida oranges are only that if grown in Florida; likewise, A Christian is only that if grown in Christ. What Christ did at Calvary should cause you to affect those he places in your path. "Before the effect, one believes in different causes than one does after the effect", *Friedrich Nietzsche.*

Chapter 2

Going in circles
(Round and Round I Go.)

"Like a dog that returns to his vomit, is a fool who repeats his foolishness", *Proverbs 26:11 AMP*. We get in trouble and ask God to help. Now God responds, and we are free from trouble, but if we return to the same trouble again, we are going in circles. Imagine a person in a relationship who learns that the relations in this ship are not profitable for either party. There may be lying, cheating, abuse, or threats to life. You cry out to God in desperation for help. Okay, God responds, freeing you from that. What do you do with this newfound freedom? You give it back. Yes, you go back to that same situation that you were just delivered. You're just going in circles. "Stand fast therefore in the liberty wherewith Christ hath made us free, and be not entangled again with the yoke of bondage" *Galatians 5:1 KJV*. One who intentionally hurts and is destructive towards us is an enemy, not one who loves us. If it fights, bites, scratches, or harms you in any way, it is not love; it seeks not your greatest good.

You have been in bondage for so long; it is what feels right to you.
This newfound freedom is unknown to you; you fear the unknown.
Israel said unto Moses, because there were no graves in Egypt, hast thou taken us away to die in the wilderness? Wherefore, hast thou

dealt thus with us, to carry us forth out of Egypt? Is not this the word that we did tell thee in Egypt, saying, let us alone, that we may serve the Egyptians? For it had been better for us to serve the Egyptians, than that we should die in the wilderness, *Exodus 14:11-12 KJV*. They were willing to return to what they were delivered from because they feared the unknown. They had no idea how GOD was to help them out of their situation; what they forgot was that God had freed them. This quote reminded me of what happened later in this story: "I told her I'd wait forever for her, but that was before I found somebody else who'd give me a ride home," *Jarod Kintz*. As you will read later in this story, *Exodus 32*, while Moses was on the mountain receiving the law from GOD, they yielded to impatience and did their own thing. God's chosen people kept going in circles and allowed satan to deceive them through their impatience to sin against God by making a "*golden calf*" idol god. Remember, they were free from these things; returning to leadership that worships idols is the same as returning to bondage (*Going in circles*).

We are sight walkers by default (*something we can touch and see clearly; tangible proof*), not faith walkers (*those who believe what GOD has already done is proof enough*). We tend to be more confident in the tangible. The people of Jesus' time saw and knew Him, but not all were confident, and some lacked faith in Him. Was this because He talked about a GOD that has yet to make Himself tangible? What was Jesus? The Word of God in the flesh! We fear that which is unseen and unknown. Israel refuses to go into the land because of fear, *Deuteronomy 1*, and *Numbers 14*. They went back and forth with belief and then unbelief, going in circles. Do they not remember that they were slaves in Egypt? Do they not remember crying out to GOD for deliverance? You can't go back to your old life; there is nothing there but bondage. We walk in circles because darkness prevents us from seeing the path. "And this is the condemnation, that light is come into the world, and men loved darkness rather than light, because their deeds were evil", *John 3:19 KJV*. Some even see darkness as their friend; they feel darkness understands them better than light because light exposes things about them that lead to judgment, and darkness doesn't judge them. Well, darkness doesn't have to because it already has them denying who or what they can become in the light. Darkness has no power over light, only over you; this is why light expels darkness. When the light comes, darkness is no longer seen in full effect, only shadows, reminding us that it is still there. "For the light to shine so brightly, the darkness must be present", *Francis Bacon*. Darkness is sin, and light represents the awareness that darkness is always there but under control.

Adversity is a state, condition, or instance of serious or continued difficulty. "Adversity is like a strong wind. It tears away from us all but the things that cannot be torn, so that we see ourselves as we really are", *Arthur Golden.* Some of us have lived with dark deeds for so long that our lives have adjusted to the darkness, just as our eyes will adjust to darkness after being absent from the light; it deceives us into believing we are gaining ground, but we are just going in circles.

His ways are subtle and cause changes that are difficult to perceive or understand. Some are so fine, delicate, or faint that you don't notice the changes until someone brings them to your awareness.

Some are unaware of their dark deeds; it's just their way, as they understand it. *Example*: If you go to a Coinstar machine, you will see a few bags on the side of the machine that were used to carry the coins, but there is usually a trash can nearby. Dark thinking (*lazy, sorry, whichever*) tells them to toss the bag on the side of the machine. *Psalms 119:105* states that the word leads us out of darkness. Many live in darkness because they seek the wrong god: *2 Corinthians 4:4 KJV* "In whom the god of this world hath blinded the minds of them which believe not, lest the light of the glorious gospel of Christ, who is the image of God, should shine unto them". The followers of this god want all that this world has to offer and then some. So, if you are still blinded by deception, then you believe not. Are you who you thought you were?

"The phrase "god of this world" (*"god of this age"*) indicates that satan is the major influence on the hopes, opinions, ideas, goals, and views of the majority. He influences the world's commerce, education, and philosophy. The thoughts, ideas, speculations, and false religions of this world are from his influences, control, and have sprung from his lies and deceptions", *unknown.* Things such as same-sex marriage, a foolish and a wise man can obtain a Gun permit; integrity is not the major requirement desired for the leader of a nation. Lawlessness will come, but the beast will only hold power because [*2 Thessalonians 2:9-12*] God will allow it for a time, but when that time is up, then comes the judgment. Discernment of worldly power: *Daniel 7* equips believers to view political systems realistically—as temporary, often beastly, yet overseen by providence. Apostasy comes first [that is, the great rebellion, the abandonment of the faith by professed Christians], and the man of lawlessness is revealed.

Our first use of freedom outside of the circle should be to seek & know what God expects from us to keep us from going in circles. Look at it this way: If we look back at the old Batman and Superman TV series we thought were so awesome as kids, they now seem so fake because we are outside of the circle, now, looking in; we are now seeing with wisdom. Let me make it simple. We sometimes act like a person struggling to keep from drowning, in a panic, struggling, desiring someone to save them, they are only in three feet of water, and all they have to do is stand up. God said, "Turn to me with all your heart" *Joel 2:12-13 KJV*. Our focus now should be on submitting to His will. Focus on the will of GOD sets us free. *John 8:32 KJV* "And ye shall know the truth, and the truth shall make you free".

Circle dwellers spend so much time in the circle that things begin to look different within. "Just because everything is different doesn't mean anything has changed", *Irene Peter.* We work the jobs WE work to make the money WE want, to afford the things WE want, but at the same time, WE are unhappy, and continue to seek more. WE keep doing it over and over (*going in circles*). WE only need the things

WE want because WE want to need them (*worldly influence*). Now that you have climbed the ladder of success, your lifestyle will change; you can now afford things. This keeps you in the circle, now you have to keep doing the same thing over and over, to keep this lifestyle you feel you deserve. "For it is [not your strength, but it is] God who is effectively at work in you, both to will and to work [that is, strengthening, energizing, and creating in you the longing and the ability to fulfill your purpose] for His good pleasure", *Philippians 2:13 AMP.*

"They are from the world and therefore speak from the viewpoint of the world, and the world listens to them", *John 4:5 NIV*. Some people care more about the brand of a thing than they do about their character; they can't stand anybody; can't get along with anybody, but they are sporting the latest fashions. There are probably more times than not that fear robs us of happiness; fear keeps us going in circles; we fear losing that source of income that affords these things we desire, at least, this is the way we see it. Fear and peace cannot coexist; in fact, fear robs you of peace. You can only conquer fear outside of the circle; in other words, you're like a hamster on a wheel, running, but going nowhere.

"Since you became alive again, so to speak, when Christ arose from the dead, now set your sights on the rich treasures and joys of heaven where he sits beside God in the place of honor and power. Let heaven fill your thoughts; don't spend your time worrying about things down here. You should have as little desire for this world as a dead person does. Your real life is in heaven with Christ and God. And when Christ, who is our real life, comes back, you will shine with him and share in all his glories. Away then with sinful, earthly things; deaden the evil desires lurking within you; have nothing to do with sexual sin, impurity, lust, and shameful desires; don't worship the good things of life, for that is idolatry. God's Terrible Anger Is Upon Those Who Do Such Things", *Colossians 3:1-5 TLB.* God has provided an opening for you to leave the circle, but we sometimes cannot see it. We are beginning to enjoy going in circles, just as much as a kid on a carousel; never wanting it to end, having fun, and enjoying life. This should lead us to pray. We should ask the Holy Spirit to help us see past our spiritual blindness. Spiritual blindness prevents us from seeing that we are not who we thought we were. We should pray for clarity in our understanding that GOD orders our steps. GOD helps us to follow his ordered steps; this is how we get out of the circle. GOD closes the doors that we keep focusing on, those doors that lead to affliction, pain, hopelessness, etc. We should pray to GOD for help in seeing the open door He provided for us to leave the circle. Awareness is the key to the truth, and the truth will set you free.

Chapter 3

Smarter than the average bear
(The Yogi Bear Syndrome)

The average person sees themselves as Yogi Bear did: "smarter than the average bear." We all know that Yogi wasn't as crafty as he believed himself to be. Boo Boo (*the sidekick*) was a critical thinker, and that saved them each time. This is most of us at certain times in our lives. God does things for us that we fail to recognize; this leads us to believe that we did it, but in fact, we deserve no credit. God is all-knowing; God has a purpose for us and gives us what we need to carry out the task given. "Trust in the LORD with all thine heart; and lean not unto thine own understanding. In all thy ways acknowledge him, and he shall direct thy paths. Be not wise in thine own eyes: fear the LORD, and depart from evil", *Proverbs 3:5-7 KJV*. When we believe we are "smarter than the average bear", we leave God out. This is why we do dumb things that we think are smart while responding to human wisdom. Just as Yogi believed he was all that, sometimes we see things the same way Yogi did.

Perception is not always reality; are you who you thought you were?

When we were growing up, we did dumb things we thought were so brilliant, but our parents often knew what we were about to do before we did it. Why? Because they knew us better than we knew ourselves, it is the same with God. We thought we were fooling them because we were so slick; a good parent would counter our actions before we started to prevent harm to us; a good parent sometimes would help us behind the scenes to achieve good things, but we would find out later, but for a few moments...we thought we had it going on, this also is the same with God. Often, we are led by what we choose not to believe rather than what we believe; perception is not always reality. Are you who you thought you were? If reading this raises awareness that we do need God's guidance, then good, because awareness is the key to the truth, and the truth shall set you free. "True wisdom comes to each of us when we realize how little we understand about life, ourselves, and the world around us", *Socrates.*

We often lie to ourselves, allowing satan (*the devil*) to alter our way of thinking; the perception of his suggestion seems to become our new reality; since we are "smarter than the average bear" and on top of our game, the subliminal suggestion appears to come from our thoughts. We are astute and "smarter than the average bear". Once your way of thinking is compromised, you begin to make bad choices, which have consequences, and those consequences are more than you thought they would be because you did not consider the consequences when you chose to do what you did. "We can evade reality, but we cannot evade the consequences of evading reality", *Ayn Rand*. God does not protect us from consequences derived from our foolishness [*you participate in questionable or illegal activities; you get busted; have the church praying all night for your release from jail; take up money for your bail. Remember, whatsoever you sew, you reap*], Galatians 6:7.

When we tell ourselves it is only a tiny sin, we lie to ourselves. "Therefore to him that knoweth to do good, and doeth it not, to him it is sin", *James 4:17 KJV*. If you believe it is a sin and you know a better way and choose not to exercise the other option, then it is a sin. You know, when you get that haunting spirit before a fall. If we tell ourselves that playing the lottery is not the same as gambling because it is legal, we lie to ourselves. Betting money or valuables and often participating in games of chance is considered gambling. If there is a chance to win, there is a chance to lose. You play over and over, hoping for that chance to win or exhaust all your resources; the win becomes the driving force, and you are no longer relying on God for your needs, but on chance. Now, the addiction set in with everybody but you, knowing it. Wait! You are "smarter than the average bear", and you have a plan, and you have skills. Even with skills, you lose sometimes, and every loss, gives cause to continue playing, and the cycle goes on. Perception is not always reality; are you who you thought you were? "We are so accustomed to disguise ourselves to others, that in the end, we become disguised to ourselves", *François La Rochefoucauld*. This is not to say you won't sin because *Ecclesiastes 7:20* states: "For there is not a just man upon earth, that doeth good, and sinneth not". Good is not all he does; weakness and ignorance occasionally cause him to sin, but not willingly.

"He that covereth his sins shall not prosper: but whoso confesseth and forsaketh them shall have mercy", *Proverbs 28:13 KJV*. "If anyone sins deliberately by rejecting the Savior after knowing the truth of forgiveness, this sin is not covered by Christ's death; there is no way to get rid of it. There will be nothing to look forward to but the terrible punishment of God's awful anger, which will consume all his enemies", *Hebrews 10:26-27 TLB*. Many will not agree with these truths, but hopefully, you will still profit from them. "When I disagree with a rational man, I let reality be our arbiter. If I am right, he will learn: if I am wrong, I will: one of us will win, but both will profit", *Ayn Rand*. Awareness is the key to the truth, and the truth will set your mind free.

The nonbelievers see neon lights around our indiscretions, causing them to perceive some believers as hypocrites, but David is known as a man after God's own heart (*1 Samuel 13*). After David realized he was not who he thought he was, he turned his heart fully to

God. Perception is not always reality; are you who you thought you were? "I am the wisest man alive, for I know one thing, and that is that I know nothing", *Socrates*. Haman (*Ester 6 & 7*) thought he was "smarter than the average bear". Haman hangs on the gallows that he had constructed for Mordecai. satan deceives to destroy. satan got Haman to commit himself to a course of action he thought would achieve his aims, but it destroyed him instead. "He who thinks he is raising a mound may only in reality be digging a pit", *Ernest Bramah*. "Whoso diggeth a pit shall fall therein: and he that rolleth a stone, it will return upon him", *Proverbs 26:27 KJV*.

Ask yourself how I got to this place in my life; why did I arrive at the point of believing that what I am doing is okay? Is it just what I observed from those surrounding me as I grew up doing things the way they did? Was their behavior due to not knowing a better way, or just how they chose to behave? Some may have known better ways, but getting them to the point of believing that the alternative way is better than what they are doing is an almost impossible task. Most of them probably did not want to be labeled as the other, different from the majority, not a member of the village, etc.

"Our human tendency is to be impatient with the person who cannot see the truth that is so plain to us. We must be careful that our impatience is not interpreted as condemnation or rejection", *Henry B. Eyring*. Just remember, Love always seeks better ways to manifest itself. The royal law is to love your neighbor as yourself, regardless of who your neighbor is. We are more at home with those who are like us than with those who are not. "Birds of a feather flock together." *unknown*. We must pray that we are not flocking with those whose actions are the opposite of love because that action is wrong. If we are flocking with them, we are or will become like them, and even if we are not as they are, we will be behaving like one of them. This is not to say that if a bear spends all its life around tigers, it will become a tiger, but rather, a bear with tiger-like tendencies. Since love is seeking the greatest good of another, love will help to understand why they do what they do. Seeking their greatest good of another means finding methods that will help them become better at approaching things satan throws at us to keep our focus away from the things of God."There's too much tendency to attribute to God the evils that man does of his own free will", *Agatha Christie*.

Those who believe themselves to be smarter than the average bear are victims of deception. The type of deception that leads to the belief that there is a reward for walking in darkness. They believe they can outsmart God by living as they please until that dying day. On their deathbed, they confess their sins and ask God for forgiveness; they get the best of both worlds without giving up anything. Well. God knows your heart and intentions, and you are not that smart. God knows that with most people it is all about what things look like, rather than what they are; they'll be doing the wrong things, but looking good while they are doing it. Perception is not always reality.

As for darkness; some walk in darkness knowingly, they do somewhat believe in the return of Jesus Christ; they want to remain in darkness because; they do agree that the children of light will be taken after the dead in Christ. They want to be the remaining; so they can keep living as they are. They believe that after this, they can just wave their hands in the air, and party like they just don't care until the end of time. Well, that's not how it will be, sorry! There will still be consequences for your actions. "For it is written, a*s* I live, saith the Lord, every knee shall bow to me, and every tongue shall confess to God", *Romans 14:11 KJV*. "By myself I have sworn, my mouth has uttered in all integrity a word that will not be revoked: Before me every knee will bow; by me every tongue will swear", *Isaiah 45:23 KJV*. When we read about the end events in Revelation, our desire to be the remaining might change.

We must consciously choose what we want to become, do we want to be smarter than the average bear or just smart enough to know we need God? Freedom comes with understanding who you are. If you have been told all your life, that you; are never going to be anything but bad news, then, you don't know who you are and are bound by that. When Christ takes over your life; show you things you can become through His spirit, and that you can do all things that He set out for you to do through Him that strengthens you, then you become to know who you are, and freedom comes from that. Awareness is the key to the truth, and the truth will set you free.

Knowing and understanding who we are should be enough to discourage our thoughts of being smarter than the average bear. I believe God allowed Man to go into space for him to look back and see the vastness of where he lives, but also, to see how tiny the earth is from afar. This should allow him to see how great God is and how little we are; in both respects: how small we are compared to the earth and God; looking closer to home, imagine yourself in the middle of an ocean; you are not even visible from the sky unless you create something bigger than yourself that identify your position. Awareness is the key to the truth, and the truth will set your mind free.

Chapter 4

It is what it is
(*Perception is not always reality*)

"Superman is, after all, an alien life form. He is simply the acceptable face of invading realities", *Clive Barker*. Superman, as we know, was a hero with a mission to help mankind; to be a protector, and to save those that needed saving. Jesus was a man with a mission: helping mankind, protecting, and saving those who need saving. Both would be considered aliens; neither is from this planet. Jesus was born on Earth, but conceived from a heavenly source. Superman, though from Krypton, was raised on Earth by parents chosen by his father, and likewise was Jesus. They were being advised by their non-earthly fathers, being in constant contact with them. Superman had to fly to his safe place ["fortress of solitude"], then insert a crystal into a pacific place to see a hologram of his father, speaking to him with a message of encouragement. Jesus didn't have to do all that; all He had to do was pray to His Father, but that was for our sake, teaching us how to communicate with God. He and the Father are one, therefore not truly separated, but for the moment He laid down His life, reuniting when He picked it up again.

Superman wanted people to know him as Superman when they needed him; otherwise, he disguised himself as Clark Kent because of man's well-known behavior towards those who are not like him. It is funny how man is quick to judge someone who is not like him until that one becomes a hero to them. In other words, man will use you for what he needs, and after that, you are a threat to him because you are different. I'm glad that man didn't make me, I'm just saying. Superman was aware that if people knew him as both, they would feel threatened and attempt to rid themselves of him, just as they did during the Salem witch trials against known and suspected witches (*becoming vigilantes for God, as they saw it*). Saul, before the Damascus road experience, believed himself to be a vigilante for God. If we spend as much time seeking the greatest good of another, as we do seeking to judge another (*as if we are all that*) because; they are not like us (*sometimes that's a good thing*); maybe we can truthfully say that another enjoys our company because; we don't judge them, we only seek their greatest good; we point them towards things that is in their best interest; we point them away from the wrong things (*presenting a better way*) they were doing without telling them that they were doing wrong. This is easier for them to see without believing we are judging them, and we don't look like hypocrites. Judging another for whatever habit they may indulge in, pretending to be better than them, makes you worse off, as you judge them to be; you may not indulge in what they do, but you're doing something that diminishes your ability to judge; in other words, you dropped that stone you were ready to throw, *John 8:6-7. Romans 12* says the Christian life is a life of total dedication and service to others. It is what it is.

When Jesus was on earth, He was God in the flesh (*The word of God in living color*); He was more like God who disguised Himself as Jesus; the people were excited about His arrival; they had awaited His arrival with the understanding that He would end all their troubles; they believed Him to be the type of savior superman was to those in that fictional story, a hero. His mission was different. He was here to save lost souls, but, like Superman, He gave hope to mankind; they had someone to look to for salvation. Superman had a weakness: kryptonite, a substance from his home planet; he was also weakened by his love, caring for mankind, regardless of how they would accept him if they knew the truth. His enemies would use mankind (*his weakness*) to throw him off of their trail; they would capture someone and dare him to rescue them and stop a crime at the same time, knowing his loyalty was to saving mankind, the evil-doer would attempt to put a yoke (*caring for a people that will throw you under the bus when something better comes along*) around his neck.

Jesus is not weakened, but strengthened by something from his heavenly home (*The Holy Spirit*), still, love and caring for mankind is his mission (*teaching people to care for one another with unconditional love*), not his weakness, unlike Superman, Jesus wanted the world to know His true identity; the people rejected that and killed him, not knowing that He came here to die for them anyway because; he loves us that much. Superman is fiction, Jesus is real. It is what it is.

When we are burdened with a yoke around our neck, the yoke is not visible to all. I mean, there's not a physical yoke about our neck, but our condition plus troubles and things we go find to worry about, etc, this is our yoke. These things are as burdensome as a physical yoke on the oxen; they control us just as the yoke on the oxen. It is used to control the oxen. The yoke could also be your desire to be judged by others, you know: when you do things to please others to receive what you consider positive judgment, you want their approval. Now, you know that if you thought no one cared about your position in life, you wouldn't do half the things you do to control their opinion of you. It is what it is.

Some yokes, we believe, are part of our attire because we have worn them for so long, it has us to the point that we have accepted it and believe that this is just how it is to be. God is aware of the yoke about the neck; He will remove the yoke and destroy it when He knows we are truly ready for it to be removed; when we receive the influences of the Holy Spirit; when we learn to truly cast our cares at His feet, and leave them there, and not return to collect them again because; we found a better and quicker way to deal with these problems ourselves.

Do you ever wonder why it appears you can't get ahead? It appears as though everything you touch turns to dust, not gold. Your perception is: God is not seeing your struggles. So it appears. If you noticed, the word "appears" was used; well, that's because perception is not always reality. God, in His infinite wisdom, sees far more than we. Remember, His ways are not our ways; His thoughts are not our thoughts; His desire is for us to be free from the distractions of temptations. In *Matthew 6*, He taught us to pray, "lead us not into temptation". Keep this in mind when seeking more: sometimes, more means greater temptations. Why would a kind, caring, and loving God put you in the path of temptation? *1 Corinthians 10:13* tells us: we will not be tempted beyond what we can bear. satan will, of course, try to push beyond those limits, hoping to break you down, but the same scripture states that God will also make a way for you to escape. Sometimes, the struggle is where you need to be; it is God allowing what you need. It is what it is.

Superman was told by his father that he would be a symbol of good. Jesus was already a symbol of good. Superman's father told him he would be like a god to the people on Earth; only those who truly believed God saw Jesus as God. Because there are people who will not read the Bible, we have to represent, just as Superman and Jesus did; we might be the only Bible they will read, and they must see God in us. We will not be perfect, but at least we can give them the best example of what it is to know God, it is what it is.

Strange as it may seem, the casinos are the way the church should be [in a sense]. At the casino, you will see a variety of people, of all races, healthy, lame, impotent, some even in what appears to be a hospital bed; some in wheelchairs with oxygen tanks while smoking a cigarette, rich, poor, believers, nonbelievers, preachers, and pastors. The only thing that you don't see (*if so, it is in small quantities*) is judgment. If you see someone in what appears to be a hospital bed that somehow pushed away from the machine, you give them a push back up to the machine and keep on rolling. If you are seated next to someone of a different race, you keep playing your game without interruption. The small quantity of judgment lies between smokers and nonsmokers, but they now have separate sections. Overall, the reason for no judgment is that they are all there for the same reason; they are all gamblers on one accord, hoping to win the big one.

This is sad to say, and detrimental to the church, but true. In the church, all are not on one accord; not there for the same reason; some for true worship; some for the fashion show; some to see what they can see and be seen; negative judgment is there also, some won't sit next to someone just because they are different, and at church, you will see the lame, impotent and also some in what appears to be a hospital bed, but they will not receive the same care and compassion they would at the casino; they will receive a lot of strange looks, from people that are supposed to be practicing love; quite a few members will not sit near them for fear of having to care for them, We are our brother's keeper. Don't let satan fool you into thinking the church is bad news because it's not. Charge it to the nonbeliever assembling amid the believer; placed there by satan to deter anyone with a desire to do good; encouraging them to believe it is worthless to do so (*Deception*). There are real believers in the assembly; they have yet to reach the point of living in ways that draw one toward change. Then, some say they believe, but their actions prove otherwise. They dress in questionable ways; clothes (*or lack thereof*) that draw much attention (*vanity*), with attitudes from hell itself; this makes the elders fearful of telling them the truth. Well, *Titus 2* states that you still must teach them (*after much prayer*) because, if you don't, satan will continue to teach them his way. satan is working his angles now, to put the son of perdition into place; the one that opposes and exalts himself above all that is called God, or that is worshiped, so that he sits as God in the temple of God, showing himself that he is God. *2 Thessalo-*

nians 2 Many will fall away because; they received not the love of the truth, that they might be saved. It is what it is.

5

Chapter

Self-Inflicted Wounds
("Be not deceived; God is not mocked: for whatsoever a man soweth, that shall he also reap", *Galatians 6:7 KJV.*)
By: David Harris & Chris Johnson

The questions: Who, What, Why, & How are the primary focus of the assessment? Who are you? What are you doing? Why are you doing it? How are you doing it?

"Do not wish to be anything but what you are, and try to be that perfectly", *St. Francis Desales (about a life of integrity is my take on this).* You are the person who loves you. If you are not, you should be. Learning to love oneself can be difficult for some due to the puppet master syndrome. You have been controlled (*dictated living*) for so long without your knowledge of the strings attached; you believe you are who "*they*" say you are. For too long, you have wanted to (*some coveted*) be what "*they*" are, and you forget who you are. **Who are you?** Are you who you thought you were? You just might be better than you think, and "*they*" envy you. *Envy: resentful awareness of an advantage enjoyed by another.* If you believe Jesus is who He says He is and God raised Him from the dead, then you have been made alive by Jesus Christ because God loves you that much; through an act of kindness, He made salvation available to you by grace through faith, *Ephesians 2*.

What are you doing? Refusing to tell yourself that you do not love yourself, you love what "*they*" are, causing you to spend much time trying not to be you. The things you have done to yourself that have caused you harm [*some wounds you are not aware of*] are self-inflicted wounds. You chose to do them, and even if "*they*" did it to themselves, "*they*" did not do it to you without you allowing them control. You are giving others control over you. "Worse than telling a lie is spending your whole life staying true to a lie", *Robert Brault*. "All of us also lived among them at one time, gratifying the cravings of our flesh and following its desires and thoughts. Like the rest, by nature we were deserving of wrath. But because of his great love for us, God, who is rich in mercy, made us alive with Christ even when we were dead in transgressions—it is by grace you have been saved. And God raised us with Christ and seated us with him in the heavenly realms in Christ Jesus", *Ephesians 2:3-6 NIV*.

Why are you doing it? Because of the vampire syndrome, you are cursed to suck the blood from another for your survival; you drain the life from others with your issues that are direct results of wounds that are self-inflicted. You sleep while it is day, avoiding the Son (*light*), and creep as the children of (*Darkness*) night, trying to avoid the cross. Lifting the curse could make it hard to look into the mirror, keep looking until the vampire syndrome is gone, and the truth is looking back at you, and discover that it is a self-inflicted wound. Whatever you sow, you also reap. You believe that choosing not to be you is not your fault. "We must be willing to let go of the life we planned so as to have the life that is waiting for us", *Joseph Campbell*. "For we are God's handiwork, created in Christ Jesus to do good works, which God prepared in advance for us to do", *Ephesians 2:10 NIV*.

How am I doing this? Well, while giving excuses to place blame upon others, truth be told, the worst enemy you have faced just might be you; that is a softball-sized pill to swallow. "It's a hard thing to discover that what you've always wanted is of no value to you at all." *Unknown.* But this truth brings you to the point of discovering that being like someone else is not you.

A profound statement was made that took a moment to absorb the significance of this statement: "Manhood and discipline are the same. To be a real man means you are willing to accept the responsibilities and the accountability that come with that title, and you must have the discipline to position yourself to meet those responsibilities", *Unknown.*

It is so simple, yet complicated. The inability to sacrifice what we do for what we know we need to do. To see how we can rationalize our decisions to do what we want, until those choices might blow up in our faces. It's amazing. Then, we blame everyone and everything associated with the failure except ourselves for making the wrong decision in the first place. **How are you doing this?** You are sacrificing yourself for all but what you need. You are reaping the seeds that you have sewn. Don't let your understanding be darkened; don't allow others to lead you into alienation from the life of God through ignorance because of the blindness in their hearts.

Proverbs 3 KJV "Inherent within the human heart is a longing for peace, love, and joy. Among Christians and non-Christians alike, the desire is the same. Yet peace, love, and joy do not answer just any 'beck and call". They will come only through certain means; they are fruits on the tree of wisdom. Wisdom will bring length of days (*v. 2*), peace (*v. 2*), favor with God and man (*v. 4*), strength to your bones (*v. 8*), honor (*v. 16*), pleasantness (*v. 17*), paths of peace (*v. 17*), confidence in life (*v. 26*), and freedom from the snares of life (*v. 29*), oppression (*v. 31*), and shame (*v. 35*). We all long for the benefits of wisdom. We must remember that she comes with a price: submission to the will of God and the truth of Scripture." *Crosswalk.com.*

The decision you make today will affect where you are tomorrow. To whom much is given, much is required. Those who know what is right and still choose to do wrong will be judged differently from those who do not know the difference. We have no excuses; no one to blame; we cannot claim ignorance or a lack of support, encouragement, certainly not a lack of opportunities. The only thing we lack is focus and self-discipline. *Whatsoever a man soweth, only that shall he reap; the end preexists in the means.*

The first step in reversing this trend of mediocrity is to help others avoid this fate by sharing some of your mental pitfalls, encouraging discretion in their actions, and critical thinking. You must know who you are and what you are about. Be honest with yourself about why you do the things you do; you can understand the motivating factors behind your actions. Ask yourself what you value about the effect your conduct has on others, good or bad. Sin is self-destructive; righteousness is self-constructive. "Let no corrupt communication proceed out of your mouth, but that which is good to the use of edifying, that it may minister grace unto the hearers" *Ephesians 4:29 KJV*.

The person with an addiction to whatever the addiction is arrives at that point due to a decision they made earlier in life. For example, too much alcohol destroys the liver. Even though alcohol can cause this to happen, this is a self-inflicted wound. You chose to drink it in excess, knowing the possible outcome, and the result is what it is: a self-inflicted wound.

Some people choose to believe the teachings in the Bible are old and outdated, meant only for those who lived during that era; many still live by this type thinking today because we now live according to the NEW NORMAL, where your preferred way of life is different from what was previously the norm, you now believe you should have rights and equality because you chose to live a lifestyle that was not God's plan for your life, but this is not to say you should be treated unfairly. There is no sin in being different, but some preferred ways are not aligned with God's principles. What we choose to believe in error inflicts wounds upon us. There is a misconception concerning Faith or belief; "Faith has been defined as believing despite there being nothing to believe or believing despite the evidence to the contrary. It is often paralleled with wishful thinking, especially with those who don't know God, but have been told 'ask and you shall receive'; if we believe hard enough, this idea indicates that some believe God is a genie or the wish master; we can make something come true (*regardless of whether or not God may approve*). None of these concepts is biblical. Faith is a belief based on sufficient evidence (*proof*). In other words, faith is trusting what God has revealed in His Word and, in the world, both of which give ample testimony to the truth" *Crosswalk.com*. If we fail to live the life before the unbeliever that draws them towards change, we fail to do what we were called to do; yes, we are good at telling them that if they don't change, they're going to Hell, but that's not good enough. We are to present a better way by letting our light shine on the path so they might see how we go. If you can't introduce an alternative way, just be silent."Better to remain silent and be thought a fool, than to speak out, and remove all doubt." *Abraham Lincoln.*

If your children live a life of crime, and you know this because you have bailed them out of jail several times, your house now belongs to the bail bondsman, [self-inflicted wounds]. You reap only what you sow. If they don't see Faith and Strength in you (faith that God will back you on your decision to let them stay in jail because they did commit the crime) (*whatsoever a man soweth, that shall he also reap; the end preexists in the means*), and strength to not go back on your word), they will never desire to change because; they know you will always rescue them. They need exposure to an alternative way of thinking. "To the man who only has a hammer, everything he encounters begins to look like a nail", *Abraham Maslow.*

According to history, past generations of Christians have been guilty of judging other people in excess, people who didn't share their ideology. Burning (*vigilantes helping God, I guess*) people at the stake that they (*unfairly judged*) believe to be witches is an example, but looking closer than the very distant past; look at the great prejudice that exists after the slavery period that divided the people; (*not to say division doesn't still exist*) prejudice is a self-inflicted wound and does not bring anyone closer to where they need to be when God calls their end. "Prejudice is a great time saver; you can form opinions without having to get the facts," *E. B. White*. Today, we live in an age of greater understanding, where wrong things (*a more sophisticated method of prejudice*) are more acceptable; these, too, can cause self-inflicted wounds. For example, the Bible is clear on sin and what the consequences are, but some believers today allow these things to remain unchallenged for whatever reason. The Bible warns that human hearts are deceitful (*Jeremiah 17:9*) and that trying to escape reality is often a form of self-deception, as God is not fooled (*Galatians 6:7-8*).

Hebrews 13:8 states: "Jesus the same yesterday, today, and forever". He is the same; His teachings are the same, and most of us are the same, remaining unchanged. His teaching will be the same until we change. Then, we will see more meaning in His teachings. "Love is the only force capable of transforming an enemy into a friend", *Martin Luther King, Jr*. Awareness is the key to the truth, and the truth will set you free.

6

Chapter

Dictated Living
(*The puppet syndrome*)

We often complain about leadership, rules, and guidelines, yet we seek the thing we desire to change. Aren't the rules and procedures set by a leader and, in some cases, agreed upon by the people under that leader? The very one we elect to lead us (*those who had the opportunity to elect*) is sometimes the one we reject; In fact, most of us want to do things our way, but with a leader (*someone else to blame*). Since the beginning, people have sought leadership, often rejecting the leaders who have the people's best interests at heart. It seems that when the opposite leader is in power, the people follow that leader to the ends of the earth, even the one who has an extreme, inflexible pattern of grandiosity, a profound lack of empathy, and an excessive need for admiration. The one who manifests selfishness, arrogance, manipulation, and a deep sense of entitlement, often causing severe disruption when things don't go their way, but questions the one who they need to lead them.

Israel asked for a king (*a leader*); they had judges, but they wanted a king, as those around them had. These were somewhat lawless times; the judges like Gideon, Sampson, etc. (*local heroes*) kept the order of things, so to speak; they were the enforcers. God was their king through these judges, but not a king they could see; they wanted a tangible king. Who could lead better than GOD? They rejected Him; 1 *Samuel 8.* Saul broke the Law of the Lord and then offered sacrifices to the Lord; his spiritual leadership was destroyed before he was established *(1 Samuel 15).* This lets us know that there is none above falling, no matter where we are in our spiritual walk. Jesus teaches us to pray: "Do not lead us into temptation but deliver us from the evil one" *(Matthew 6:13 KJV)*. Again, Jesus says, "Watch and pray, lest you enter into temptation" *(Matthew 26:41 KJV)*. This is to say that God is the only leader who will not fall. A leader's task is to help those under them succeed. True leaders are servants of the people under their rule, seeking their greatest good, not taking advantage of others to achieve their own goals, while vocalizing frequent envy of others

In the history we were taught, we learned about countries ruled by a dictator, a single ruler of the people; some people even worshiped them to the point of dying for the leader. What the leader said was the law. Some rulers had no love for the people, only for themselves. The relationship is one-sided, focused entirely on their needs, while exercising an Inability to take accountability, and constantly redirecting the blame onto others. The children of Israel rejected God as their king in the bible days, and He loved them to the point of dying for them in the person of Jesus Christ. Today, we say: I'm glad we don't have to live like that now, or do we?. In some countries, reading the Bible was or still is against the rules. Today, in this great country, we have the freedom to read our Bibles as much as we want. The funny thing is that we won't exercise this freedom. Why? Because Judgment is what we fear, yet it is what we seek. "He who controls others may be powerful, but he who has mastered himself is mightier still", *Lao Tzu.*

We have the opportunity to read in public, but we fear what others might think (*judgment*). That's not freedom at all. Everything we do is to please someone else; we give others the power over us; we allow others to make us dependent on their opinion (*we don't stop them*).

Example: "Your house or car would be nice enough if someone you knew didn't have a better one", *Crosswalk.com*. This is just one of many things that show us how we experience dictated living. Everybody but us dictates how we live. "When I let go of what I am, I become what I might be", *Lao Tzu*.

We will never be free from dictated living; however, we must give up trying to be a believer living like an unbeliever. Instead, we should lead the unbeliever into belief so they might have the life you enjoy. *Matthew 5:14-16* states: "Ye are the light of the world". *Isaiah 10:15 KJV* says: "Shall the ax boast greater power than the man who uses it? Is the saw greater than the man who saws? Can a rod strike unless a hand is moving it? Can a cane walk by itself"?

God used the Assyrian army to perform a task; they did not know God was using them for His purpose; they bragged to themselves how good they were, but after the task, God punished them also (*Isaiah 10:13*). God is the ultimate puppet master. Be careful what you ask for; you might get exactly that (*wanting to be like others but not knowing who or what they are*). You might end up just like them; all messed up on the inside and looking good on the outside. "If you do not change direction, you might end up where you are heading", *Lao Tzu*.

Since we will always live a dictated life, "we must choose to be dictated by righteousness, which begins with the word of God; not man's counsel, which begins with I and leads to wind and chaff", *Unknown*. Be dictated by the ultimate puppet master: God. Not all leadership offers moral and spiritual guidance; some dictate the way we live (*puppet syndrome*). You do what "they" say, not knowing who "they" are (*not tangible*). We say we want tangible, but we always settle for the intangible (*they*). Who are "they"? "Most people are other people. Their thoughts are someone else's opinions, their lives a mimicry, their passions a quotation", *Oscar Wilde*. We played games as kids, such as "Simon Says". We had to do what Simon said; if not, we were ejected from the game. Well, isn't that what the world system reminds you of? The majority (*They*) is like Simon, the one giving the commands that you must follow. In the game, if the command "Simon says jump over the broom" is given, then you must jump over the broom to stay in the game. If the command "jump over the broom" is given and you jump over the broom, then you are eliminated from the game because Simon did not give this command.

Sometimes we hang onto things Simon has directed us to do, and we forget what we are supposed to do for ourselves. God wants us to strive for the things He desires for us to do; we will never reach perfection, but striving to be is what keeps us doing the will of God. If we do what God says rather than Simon's commands, we will be closer to God's desired end. "You will never achieve what you are capable of; if you're too attached to things you're supposed to let go of", *Unknown*.

In *Deuteronomy 7*, the Israelites were commanded by righteousness (*the Word of God*) to destroy everything in the land of Canaanites that would lead them to unrighteousness, but they did not. They allowed man's counsel to dictate what they should do, and that did not turn out well. Their failure to follow instructions later caused them trouble. If we are to live dictated lives, then God should be the dictator; God dictates through love, and this is why He encourages us to love one another as He has loved us. *Deuteronomy 29* tells us to trust God in His word, and *Psalms 27* tells us that if God is with us, we should not be afraid, but some don't take God at His word because they know God is not with them.

Some view lifestyles as a democracy; they believe they should be able to live however they choose, no law (*man's law or God's law*) should dictate how they live. They believe that if they desire to be whatever, they should be whatever; with no right or wrong to judge them for how they choose to live; it's their choice. Well, it is your choice; that's what free will is. The law of God is a guide to moral values; if what you do does not measure up to God's law, then He will judge you on what you choose to do. He never said that you couldn't do whatever you do. He only said, there are consequences (*The end preexists in the means*), everything He asks us not to do is for our good, and each of those things has its own natural consequence; that's just what that is.

"To be yourself in a world that is constantly trying to make you something else is the greatest accomplishment", *Ralph Waldo Emerson.* *But if* "yourself" is not a person of integrity, then maybe you should consider becoming someone else. Awareness is the key to the truth, and the truth will set your mind free.

7

Chapter

You didn't see because you were too busy looking
(The Vampire Syndrome)

Our lives could be compared to that of the old vampire movies; they were afraid of the cross, they were eternal beings, and they would drain the blood from another for their survival. They could not be exposed to the sun because of their dark nature, because light expels darkness. The vampire's weakness is the heart; when a wooden stake is driven through their heart, they go into eternal sleep until they are resurrected. The only difference with us is: that sin is the wooden stake that pierces our hearts; sin keeps us in darkness and causes us to avoid the SON *(light)* because; His light exposes what we hide in darkness and will expel it and the word of God will quicken us; sin will lead to death, and we sleep until we are resurrected to be judged for the decisions we made *(look at light and darkness this way; when facing the light, your shadow is behind you, as if darkness is following you and light is leading you. When you have the light on either side, the shadow is on the opposite side, as if light and darkness are walking on both sides. Now, when you turn your back on the light, your shadow is in front of you, as if darkness is leading you, but light is still behind you waiting for you to turn around; it is there to lead you away from darkness.)* Even then, some will say: Lord, the devil made me do it, but still, sin will prevent us from spending eternity in heaven, only sin will do that because sin stands between us and immortality.

The part that stands out the most is when a vampire looks in the mirror and sees no reflection. In some situations, we don't see ourselves as the problem or cause of the problem. We find it easier to blame everyone else. We look in that mirror and blame all that we see. It's my mother, my father, my brother, and so on; remember, we are compared to the vampire; we don't see ourselves, therefore, we are not to blame. Remember that old phrase "The Devil made Me Do It". Let us not forget that we have the freedom of choice. God judges what we choose. Right and wrong are always present simultaneously; if we choose right, we are judged for that choice; therefore, if we choose wrong, we will be judged for that choice; this is called accountability. We are to be accountable for all we do. The Bible warns us of this. *Matthew 7:3-4 KJV* states: "And why beholdest thou the mote that is in thy brother's eye, but considerest not the beam that is in thine own eye? Or how wilt thou say to thy brother, Let me pull the mote out of thine eye; and, behold, a beam is in thine own eye"? *Matthew 7:3-4 KJV.*

Saul, in *Acts 9*, did not see a reflection in the mirror; he was deceived by his beliefs, seeing what he was doing was right; he was doing the work of God, as he saw it. He was vigilant in all his efforts. But, *verse 17 KJV:* "And Ananias went his way, and entered into the house; and putting his hands on him said, Brother Saul, the Lord, even Jesus, that appeared unto thee in the way as thou camest, hath sent me, that thou mightest receive thy sight, and be filled with the Holy Ghost.", this is when Paul was able to see himself in the mirror. This is what Paul meant in *1Timothy 1:15.*

Peter, in *Acts 10*, did not see a reflection in the mirror, according to what he knew before the vision of the sheet on the rooftop; He could not see that God showed no prejudice, only the Jews did. It wasn't until his eyes were open that he was able to preach the sermon in *verses 34-43. Customs or traditions can be our worst enemy; they are just things that are usually done, not necessarily the right thing, but things.* Keep in mind, that all customs of people in the Bible were not all approved by God; this is why Jesus' teachings mostly lead you away from this way of thinking; the Pharisees' teaching was an issue based on their misunderstanding of the Law—dwelling on the externals as the source of uncleanness and not seeing that the defilements were sin in the world, not unclean things; they failed to understand the Scriptures that they taught. "Beware lest any man spoil you through philosophy and vain deceit, after the tradition of men, after the rudiments of the world, and not after Christ", *Colossians 2:8 KJV*.

David didn't see a reflection of himself in the mirror until it was made visible through God using Nathan (*the accountability switch was turned on*). *2 Samuel 12:1-7,13* "Man is least himself when he talks in his own person. Give him a mask, and he will tell you the truth", *Oscar Wilde. 2 Samuel 12* Nathan's words from God placed a mask on David, allowing him to talk as if he was not the subject. David expressed his feelings freely, as he would not have if he knew the conversation was about him *(Perception is not always reality)*. When the devil blesses you, sorrow follows, all that God had blessed David with; taking another man's wife wasn't one of them. "And David said unto Nathan, I have sinned against the LORD. And Nathan said unto David, The LORD also hath put away thy sin; thou shalt not die". God's blessing has no sorrow. We too should be able to say that it is me, blinded by my selfishness and pride; I didn't see because I was too busy looking. While we look at fault in others, our blindness to our reflection keeps us from seeing how we caused this problem; certainly, someone else is to blame. Because of our selfishness, we don't always consider others in our daily decisions. Something so simple can escape us because we are too busy looking; we don't see. For example; a person in the supermarket reading magazines, *first*: if you are not purchasing it; you are stealing; you are getting information from this product, that is for sale, without buying it, *Second*: when you finish stealing, you don't bother to put it back from which it came; you moved the item; it is your responsibility to put it back since you laid the magazine on top of the sugar in the baking aisle, you knew that was wrong, but you did it anyway; I know, some of you still don't see. *Third*: now you think of the other because it benefits you, so you say: someone else will straighten this up because that's what they get paid for (*shifting the responsibility*). In real life, you were the cause of the problem and should be accountable for your actions, not someone else. You didn't see this because you were too busy looking for someone else to blame for your lack of accountability.

"Are we faithful at something in an attempt to bring God glory, the greatest good to others, loving them by demonstrating a long-term commitment to them? Or, are we faithful only to what we want and striving after that?" *Unknown.* "Faithfulness often has to do with doing what we say we're going to do, not doing what we say we don't do. It is, being in practice what we claim to be, and it involves doing it over long periods." *Unknown.*

Our "too busy looking" should be focused on how we measure up to what God expects of us, not how we compare to others in our failing to do what is expected of us. Others would not be the cause if we learn to be accountable for our actions. Darkness is always there waiting for the light to disappear. Our shadows could be a reminder, representing a glimpse of darkness leading us away from the light. "If you do not change direction, you may end up where you are heading", *Lao Tzu.*

A whole is greater than the sum of its parts; if the parts are not what they should be, the whole suffers. If four quarters equal one dollar, then those four quarters need to focus on being quarters, not the two dimes and a nickel that is the sum of the quarter, the dimes and nickels got this, the quarter need to see a reflection of a quarter to remain effective to the whole and so forth; better or more effective as a team, combination, etc., than divided and apart. If we raise our level of accountability for what we do and the choices we make, we become more aware of our actions; awareness is the key. When we are too busy looking at others' faults, we fail to see our own. This can go on for so long that it becomes a reality in our minds that all is wrong but us. This is why Jesus warned us about judging; when we judge others, we judge ourselves. Sin is Sin, no matter who does it. If you drink, smoke, and curse, some would call you a sinner. The one who is judging you commits fornication and earns money dishonestly, but you're the sinner in their eyes. None of us can cast the first stone. This is why, through an act of kindness, God gives us grace.

What we read about the Israelites causes us to subconsciously judge them for their foolishness because it seems so clear to us that some of their actions were foolish. Yet, today, when we are confronted with temptations, it doesn't seem so clear that we seek ways to justify our foolishness; surely, no one wants to be judged by others. Awareness is the key to the truth, and the truth will set your mind free. "When I let go of what I am, I become what I might be", *Lao Tzu*.

When we suffer, experience circumstances, and have not dealt with our known weaknesses, a way of thinking that causes us to keep committing the same sin over and over, then try to justify it by saying that we are only human, humans make mistakes, we cannot, however, expect God's peace until we confess these things. Sin is: not letting go of who you thought you were, so that you follow the steps that God ordered for you. We should ask God to help us be people of Virtue: Conforming to a standard of right (*Morality*), a commendable quality or trait (*Merit*); or a beneficial quality or power of a thing (*Beneficial*). Virtue relates to your core level, your character. Your mind has settled on doing right (*settled habit of mind*), doing what God expects without thinking. Virtue is what we learn when we are in relation with God, like discovering your mate's needs through relations.

Some people desire to be like the vampire (*even though fictional*); they admire the vampire's ability to live for centuries (*as long as a vampire can avoid the sun: God's Light; because vampires represent darkness*); they admire the vampire's strength; vampires are stronger than mortal men, but all their rewards are defiled, meaning: to live for centuries got to be like punishment, there is no rest in it; knowing that for centuries; you don't know; what you look like since you have no reflection, and you have to rob another of life to survive (*suck the blood from another*); where is the reward in that. Solomon said it best: ["Better it is to have no children, and to have virtue: for the memorial thereof is immortal: because it is known with God and with men."*Wisdom of Solomon 4:1-2*]. When it is present, men take an example at it, and, when it is gone, they desire it: it weareth a crown, and triumpheth forever, having gotten the victory, striving for undefiled rewards.

It sometimes appears the ungodly thrive, take deep root in their doing, and flourish. The ungodly always seem to be doing better than the godly; at least as we see it, mainly because we focus on the wrong things. Yes, they flourish in branches for a time, just as a tree, yet not stand fast, their branches shall be shaken when the wind bloweth, and leaves and fruit fall to the ground and become meat for nothing. Awareness is the key to the truth, and the truth will set your mind free. Next time you look in the mirror, look for an ambassador for Christ; a steward of God; someone trying to get to heaven, where their true citizenship is. Awareness is the key to the truth, and the truth will set you free.

Chapter 8

Vanity
(*I know this song is about me*)

Vanity is said to be excessive belief in one's ability or attractiveness to others. It can be described as self-idolatry or rejecting God for the sake of one's image, thereby becoming divorced from the grace of God. The fear of appearing original is thus a lack of pride, but not necessarily a lack of originality. "Vanity well fed is benevolent, vanity hungry is spiteful", *Mason Cooley.*

A garage door opener was created to open garage doors; it has no other purpose. Imagine if a garage door opener could go to a store to shop for lavish gifts for itself and dress like a can opener, then its existence seems meaningless (*vanity*). We can't see ourselves unless we look into something that casts reflections. Many things cast a reflection; some are hazy, blurry, and fuzzy, but a mirror allows us to see ourselves clearly. This is what the word of God does for us; it allows us to see ourselves; clearly (*Romans 7:7*). The law was not to make us feel restricted or restrained from those pleasures we thought we enjoyed, but for us to see the vanity in what we were doing; It is like eating something that tastes so good and someone comes along and tells you what it truly is that you're eating, now, knowing what it is changes the way it taste. "Before the effect, one believes in different causes than one does after the effect", *Friedrich Nietzsche.*

There is a wide belief that God makes mistakes, what I mean by that is: *that this is not meant to be judgment by any means*, judgment being the absence of facts (*facts: being aware that you are as guilty as the one you are judging*) example: the scribes and Pharisees, in *John 8:7* may have forgotten that the women in question, just may have earned as much money from them as anyone else (*not to say this is true, just an opinion to make a point*), that this is probably why they dropped their stone so quickly. Just for thought, where was the man with whom she committed this act? People spend considerable sums of money to change their appearance, such as nose jobs, plastic surgery, wrinkle removers, hair additions, and organ enhancements. God made you the way He made you; to alter that is vanity.

"For bodily exercise (*Idolizing the body is Vanity*) profiteth little: but godliness is profitable unto all things, having promise of the life that now is, and of that which is to come", *1Timothy 4:8 KJV.* "Then I looked on all the works that my hands had wrought (*Idolizing accomplishments is Vanity*), and on the labour that I had laboured to do: and, behold, all was vanity and vexation of spirit, and there was no profit under the sun", *Ecclesiastes 2:11 KJV.*

The Word is understood by those who are receptive to it; those who are not refuse to believe it. Those who receive will see the folly in not receiving it, the understanding thereof brings more abundance to their living (*so many are taught to believe that John 10:10 concerning having life more abundantly has to do with wealth*), it enhances their way of life (*those who receive and accept the word*); it opens their eyes; it is similar to watching someone doing something dumb, they know it's dumb; you know it's dumb, but they keep doing it over and over again. They know the correct way because you and others have shown them, but they refuse to change. Now, you see, because you understand what they are missing, and this gives you a greater abundance knowing that you have grown past that stage of life; on the other hand, they refuse to see it as a means of help, but rather as a means to deny them pleasure. A greater example: you give a person a bottle opener to open a bottle, they still insist on removing the bottle cap with their teeth, to prove whatever.

"Whoever loves money never has enough (*Idolizing wealth is vanity*); whoever loves wealth is never satisfied with their income: this too is meaningless", *Ecclesiastes 5:10 NIV*. "Therefore, when thou doest thine alms, do not sound a trumpet before thee, as the hypocrites do in the synagogues and the streets (*Idolizing honor of the people is Vanity*), that they may have glory of men. Verily I say unto you, they have their reward", *Matthew 6:1-7 KJV*. "For there is a man whose labour is in wisdom, and knowledge, and equity; yet to a man that hath not laboured therein shall he leave it for his portion", *Ecclesiastes 2:21 KJV*. This is vanity and a great evil (*Idolizing the children that you leave all your goods for is Vanity, for they may blow it in a matter of days, since it's not their hard work that acquired it*). "Beware of the scribes, which desire to walk in long robes, and love greetings in the markets, and the highest seats in the synagogues, and the chief rooms at feasts (*Idolizing a title or position is vanity*); Which devour widows' houses, and for a shew make long prayers: the same shall receive greater damnation", *Luke 20:46-47 KJV*.

God is the only path to finding the meaning of life. Knowledge, wealth, pleasure, work, and popularity will not be as satisfying as knowing that you are doing what God wants you to do. The Bible refers to vanity as meaningless, wickedness, falseness, and worthlessness. These are all pointless and amount to nothing, and are worthless. Like idols, they are either made by you or chosen by you; they have no life or power of their own and can do nothing for you either, you can only do for them.

"He that hath clean hands, and a pure heart; who hath not lifted up his soul unto vanity, nor sworn deceitfully" *Psalms 24:4 KJV;* this work is not in vain; if your hands are clean and your heart is pure, vanity has no place because all you do is to please God and not yourself. "In whose eyes a vile person is contemned; but he honoureth them that fear the Lord. He that sweareth to his own hurt, and changeth not" *Psalms 15:4 KJV:* this work also is not in vain. If those things that are wicked are despised by you, to the point of you not being able to pass by them without acknowledging them and pretending you didn't see them (*same-sex marriages, contrary to divine order*). But you honor those things that please God. You are a person of your word and will keep a promise no matter what.

There was a song, performed by Nat King Cole, "Nature Boy". In that song, the words are: "The greatest thing you'll ever learn, is just love, and to be loved in return". All else we seek is vanity. When family and friends leave us, it is then that we realize: "And ever has it been known that love knows not its own depth until the hour of separation", *Khalil Gibran*. We must invest in others; when we leave them, we leave them knowing more love and that we sought their greatest good. The fact that same-sex marriage was mentioned in an earlier chapter does not indicate any dislike or hatred towards those who choose such, but the idea of such an act is what God hates, and we should also (the act, not the person). God does not hate the sinner, just the act of sin itself.

"Now faith is the assurance (title deed, confirmation) of things hoped for (divinely guaranteed), and the evidence of things not seen [the conviction of their reality—faith comprehends as fact what cannot be experienced by the physical senses]", *Hebrews 11:1 AMP.* It is a belief based on sufficient evidence. In other words, faith is trusting what God has revealed in His Word, which testifies to the truth. God will keep his word; this you must believe. We have been taught for many years that all you have to do is believe, it will happen, and don't doubt. Well, if you're not sure the one who intercedes is who He says He is, and He will always keep His promise, then your belief in your request is vanity.

"In the beginning was the Word, and the Word was with God, and the Word was God. He was in the beginning with God. All things were made through Him, and without Him, nothing was made that was made. In Him was life, and the life was the light of men. . . And the Word became flesh and dwelt among us, and we beheld His glory, the glory as of the only begotten of the Father, full of grace and truth", *John 1:1-4,14 KJV*. This states that God's word is full of grace and truth; it is evidence that is not always seen because some are blinded by the enemy, who keep things that are not true ever before them, so that they cannot believe (*deception*).

Many have been led to believe that God is a genie. Instead of rubbing a bottle, go to church, kneel, and ask Him anything, and He will grant it: *"Ask and you shall receive."* You cannot hope for things if you don't have evidence that they exist. Evidence is not always what you see; it is knowing the existence of a God, who will deliver according to your faith in Him, based on what He has already proven that He is capable of doing. You didn't know Him before you got in trouble; you only knew of Him. Therefore, you're not sure how this works; you only claim to know Him because you are in trouble, and you didn't have faith in Him before this situation, but now you do? You can only have faith if you know what you seek exists without having seen it, meaning: your belief is based on His past performances, on what you know about the object of your faith (*You know that you know, but the proof is not within reach*). If you believe in Him was life, you should also; believe that the Word became flesh and dwelt among us, you should also; believe that He is the only begotten of the Father, and that He is, and He is the rewarder of them that earnestly seek Him, not just what He can do for you today and you put Him back in the bottle until you need Him again. People have been told only half-truths for many years, being told, "Child, just pray about it." If they don't believe He is who He says He is, then praying is vanity, even if you are praying that you may truly know Him in a real way; this still requires belief. "Doubt is a pain too lonely to know that faith is his twin brother", *Khalil Gibran.*

The priests held important positions as official spiritual leaders. This is what God intended. It was to be a labor of love, a love of being men of integrity before the people of God. For the people to believe God had anything to do with the priest, they had to see God working through them. The priest survived on nothing but the blessings of God, which were executed through the people who showed them much love and respect, in return for their laboring and interceding for them. A reputation for corruption began (*Vanity*). This high position became a position of power; a struggle between the sects. The Sadducees rejected belief in the *resurrection of the dead*, which was a central tenet of the *Pharisees*. The Sadducees rejected the *Oral Law* as proposed by the Pharisees. According to the Pharisees, spilled water becomes impure through its pouring. Sadducees deny that this is sufficient grounds for impurity, and so on; hopefully, you can see where this is going. During the time of Christ and the New Testament era, the Sadducees were the aristocrats. They tended to be wealthy and held powerful positions, including that of chief priests and high priests, The Pharisees were held in much higher esteem by the common man than the Sadducees, Jesus was in constant conflict with them, He rebuked them on several occasions; in all their high-class religion, they were blind to the one thing that was most important, Jesus. They saw Him as a threat to what they were taught to believe, rather than seeing Him as the solution to their unbelief. This is vanity.

If you pour water into a glass that is already filled with liquid, does the new water sink to the bottom, or is it the first to flow out? With clear water, it is hard to tell, but, if you pour a colored liquid into a glass filled with clear water you begin to see the colored liquid take control but still watered down, not as strong as it would be; if there was no water in the glass, either way, it is easier to pour out the content and fill with new substance, the other is vanity. God prefers to fill our emptiness, not pouring continuously until the substance we chose to hang on to is gone. We cannot become new with old stuff; we must empty ourselves when we come to Him to be filled.

If man's quest for knowledge of God and His plan were as great as his knowledge of strange things, such as aliens, ancient texts that prove the bible to be wrong, or prove that God does not exist, or not as we believe, that energy could be used towards discovering who He is. *First*, not all ancient texts are necessarily true; there had to be fiction writers and storytellers even then; they didn't just appear in the new centuries, the idea came from somewhere, didn't it? It is hard to believe that those things that replace the idea of a creator who loves us, versus some alien who desires to obliterate us and steal a planet that is not ours anyway.

Just as all ancient texts were not necessarily true events, the same with those who obtain high degrees such as P.H.Ds are not always wise; smart, but not always wise; not to say all of them; just those with these types of beliefs, some are a scientist; some are of other professions; some of them will have you to believe that aliens from another galaxy or a planet in our galaxy controlled the natural disasters; gave life back to some of the dead, and some even appeared as godlike beings and infiltrated man's thought to inject their way of thinking into the mind of man. Well, this might be a disappointment to some, but it is called the influence of satan. Yes, he is an alien, and is not from this planet; he resides here but is not from here. "And the Lord said unto satan, Whence comest thou? Then satan answered the Lord, and said, From going to and fro in the earth, and from walking up and down in it", *Job 1:7 KJV*.

satan's desire to destroy any belief that expresses strong faith in God. Some events, such as someone blowing up a building, killing a lot of people, or shooting up a school full of children, are the work of satan. "Be sober, be vigilant; because your adversary the devil, as a roaring lion, walketh about, seeking whom he may devour", *1 Peter 5:8 KJV*. These events are designed to "CON" you into believing God is absent or doesn't care for your safety. Why does God allow these

NO REFLECTION, ARE YOU WHO YOU THOUGHT YOU WERE?

things? God does not protect us just because He made us; some things we cause because we are under satan's control. God's protection is for those who trust Him in faith because they believe He is who he says He is, not just some dude who comes when you call Him when you're in trouble. Believe it or not, some believe that God can be manipulated and bent to their will because they see Him as being at their beck and call. With their great worldly accomplishments and wealth, surely God has been blessing them. satan wants you to believe this, keeping you from discovering the truth. If God just protected all because He made them, then Sodom and Gomorrah wouldn't have been destroyed, and Noah wouldn't have saved only those he was given instructions to save. "Be not deceived; God is not mocked: for whatsoever a man soweth, that shall he also reap", *Galatians 6:7 KJV*. This is not to say you will reap what your brother sowed, but only what you sowed shall you reap. Sodom and Gomorrah, it's apparent they were all sowing the same thing, the same with those in Noah's day. The consequence of our foolishness, from this God, does not necessarily protect us.

God knows you; while you are praying, He knows the sincerity of your request; He knows your plan if He gives you what you ask. We believe our intentions are good and pure, but in fact, sometimes they are not. We sometimes attempt to "CON" God in prayer, "Lord, I've been REAL faithful, Lord, bless me to go to Paris for my next vacation, to enjoy the fruit of my labor that you so graciously provide me with" (*We still see ourselves as mere human beings, children of the age caring more for things of the world than the thing of God*). You want to believe that this is your motive, but subconsciously, you are thinking vanity, "the Wilsons thought they were the only ones who had gone to Paris; I can't wait to tell them we went". This took all the purity out of your motive. God saw it, but you didn't. This is how satan works; he presented this idea to you undercover; you accepted it, and it was sown; now you reap what you have sown. Don't be put out too much;

he did the same thing to Eve, but that still doesn't make it right; he's the father of lies and deception.

We who are adopted into God's family are now His children; we are newly created in Him in holiness and righteousness, by grace, through faith; we have inherited great things in heaven; wealth and power, by grace, through faith. When we begin to act, as we belong to God rather than who we were before, our faith will grow; seeking the right things for the wrong reason is vanity. Those who have degrees from higher learning and experiences bountiful lives (*as most define bountiful*) have received much more knowledge along the way. All that they have learned, understood, and wish to teach and share with others is all vanity if they can't convince others not to be anxious (*worry*), because they don't have it as they got it. "Do not be anxious *or* worried about anything, but in everything [every circumstance and situation] by prayer and petition with thanksgiving, continue to make your [specific] requests known to God", *Philippians 4:6 AMP*. Worrying will not fix the problem, nor yield a solution, but praying will, if faith is the foundation of prayer.

Anxiety is the paranoia of something out there that seems menacing but may not be; menacing, and, indeed, may not even be out there. "Neither comprehension nor learning can take place in an atmosphere of anxiety", *Rose Kennedy*.

Most consider their struggles or what they don't have, a storm (*disruption to normal conditions*); in fact, where you are might be where you are supposed to be. Most often, you have been told, "It will be all over in the morning" or "This too will pass". Well, this also is vanity. Some wait until morning to find out that things are the same as they were last night because they have been told all their lives only half of a scripture. "For his anger lasts only a moment, but his favor lasts a lifetime; weeping may stay for the night, but rejoicing comes in the morning", *Psalms 30:5 NIV*. This is not about your storm. If you had God's favor before you messed up and angered Him, then His short-lived anger is but a night; in the morning, you can rejoice to be back in his favor again. If you were not in His favor before the storm, then you are probably not after the storm. By prayer and supplication with thanksgiving, let your requests be made known unto God, that you desire to be in His favor.

Hosea 14 aligns with *Psalm 30:5*: the Lord instructed Hosea to take a wife named Gomer, who later became unfaithful to him. Though Hosea loves her steadfastly, her infidelity compounds, and she finally leaves him. Sometime later, as Hosea is walking down the street, he sees his wife being sold as a slave on an auction block. In a profound gesture of unconditional love, Hosea redeems (*buys back*) his wife and restores her to her former position of honor and comfort, as his wife. In doing so, Hosea's message warns Israel about misunderstanding the unconditional love God has for His creation. If they sin, He will judge them; but after judgment, He will restore them to His grace. This is not just about Gomer being in God's favor, but also about us being in God's favor; we are to God what Gomer was to Hosea. "Birds sing after a storm; why shouldn't people feel as free to delight in whatever remains to them?" *Rose Kennedy.* You can be grateful that after your storm *(if there is an after, that there is still you)*, you remain. Things may be lost or damaged, but you remain.

Believing the promises of God is key to overcoming. There are many things that we think we believe, but our anxiety reveals that we are not who we thought we were. If we believe, we can be at peace because we know God is true to His word. If we do not believe God is true, we will fret (*vanity*). When you are troubled, revisit the promises of Scripture. If you are trying to believe, but still struggle with weariness and unbelief, remember the prayer of the father whose son had an evil spirit: "Lord, I believe; help my unbelief!" *Mark 9:24 KJV.*

The plagues in Egypt (*Exodus 9*)

The Egyptians worshiped idol gods (*vanity*). Each plague was designed to challenge the credibility of Egyptian gods and show the vanity of your belief in them. God does the same today. Our gods are our accomplishments. There's nothing wrong with them as servants, but when we worship them, God shows vanity in worshiping them by allowing people without them to be as happy, if not happier; those who choose to worship them experience torture from the object of worship. It is almost impossible to prevent your vehicle from getting dings and scratches (*vanity is spending an absurd amount of money on them, to begin with*), especially with "tire alligators" (*discarded 18-wheeler tires*) on the roads, they can cause all kinds of havoc, and stuff falling from the back of a truck in front of you, hauling gravel the inappropriate way, or a house that insist on having foundation problems no matter what you do to prevent it, but, we still find ways to worship these objects. Again, today, God's personal mark of blessing is the fruit of the Spirit and not necessarily of the vine. Joy is found in God, not things; joy in things leads to vanity. If you resemble these things, then yes, this song is about you. Are you who you thought you were? Awareness is the key to the truth, and the truth will set you free.

Chapter 9

Greed

"He who is not contented with what he has would not be contented with what he would like to have," Socrates.

Luke 15:11-12 KJV. (11) "There was a man who had two sons. (12) The younger one said to his father, 'Father, give me my share of the estate.' So he divided his property between them". The son's initial actions are driven by selfishness, greed, and a desire for independence.

"Greed is a sin against God, just as all mortal sins, since man condemns things eternal for the sake of temporal things," *Thomas Aquinas.* Greed, also known as avarice, cupidity, or covetousness, is an excessive appetite to possess wealth, goods, or objects of abstract value to keep for oneself, far beyond the dictates of basic survival and comfort. It is a markedly high desire for and pursuit of *wealth, status,* and *power.*

As we have all heard before concerning the phrase: "making a deal with the devil," this phrase alone encourages sin, that is because if you are willing to sell your soul for financial gain, then you have gained nothing, but have lost all (*"For what is a man profited, if he shall gain the whole world, and lose his own soul? or what shall a man give in exchange for his soul? Matthew 16:26 KJV)*. You have traded eternal for temporal; only God can give eternal. "For the **love of money** is the root of all evil: which while some coveted after, they have erred from the faith, and pierced themselves through with many sorrows", *1 Timothy 6:10 KJV*. Also, read *Amos 8*.

Many have abandoned their acquaintanceship with GOD for the sake of wealth and possessions; in their opinion, GOD did not move fast enough. Now, they have given in to the dark force that encouraged them not to wait on GOD in the first place. They sold out, but they have yet to realize that sorrow follows anything given by satan, the god of this world. satan will feed into your greed; you will want more and more and more, never getting enough, but the sorrow is yet to come. Look at it this way: if something is said that will insult your decision to do what you did, then, in your anger, you will fail to see your decision as questionable; that is, your decision not to wait on God. Imagine going to a university for two years because it was a bargain; you find out now that it was not an accredited school, as it was said to be; your credits cannot transfer to an accredited school. Now, the sorrow sets in. The shortcut you took to keep more money in your pocket is the focus of the bargain(*due to greed*) instead of researching this school, praying about it, and waiting on God; now, it will cost you more money to make it right, or forfeit the time spent in that bootleg school. No gain came from this. If someone had told you this before, you would have felt insulted. *"He who is not contented with what he has, would not be contented with what he would like to have" (sense),* Socrates.

Now, when it comes to greed for status and power, the first that comes to mind is satan himself. "For thou hast said in thine heart, I will ascend into heaven, I will exalt my throne above the stars of God: I will sit also upon the mount of the congregation, in the sides of the north: I will ascend above the heights of the clouds; I will be like the most High, *Isaiah 14:13-14 KJV* ". Let it be known that some believe Isaiah was referring to the king of Babylon, not satan, but either way, it is greed. *"Let your* conversation *be* without covetousness; *and be* content with such things as ye have: for He hath said, I will never leave thee, nor forsake thee, *Hebrews 13:5 KJV".*

As a secular psychological concept, greed is, similarly, an inordinate *desire* to acquire or possess more than one needs. This degree of inordinate is related to the inability to control the reformulation of "wants" once desired "needs" are eliminated. "Greed is a bottomless pit which exhausts the person in an endless effort to satisfy the need without ever reaching satisfaction", *Erich Fromm.* "Don't wear yourself out trying to get rich. Be wise enough to know when to quit, *Proverbs 23:4 NLT".* Greed is typically used to criticize those who seek excessive material wealth, although it may apply to the need to feel *excessively moral, social,* or otherwise *better than* another. Now that we know what greed is, are you who you thought you were?

If you observe a dog at feeding, you will discover; that even though you have given the dog something to eat, and you put more food down, the dog will either leave the food it is eating to get what you just added, to assure that it obtain all of what is now available, or try to eat both choices at the same time. The more you add, the more it will try to consume outside of what was originally given (*excess beyond its needs*). If there are two or more dogs, the alpha will be the greediest of all, running to and fro, hoping to obtain all before any other can feed from what was provided, but at the same time, protecting what it first received. It is easy to understand why dogs behave this way; they cannot reason as humans do. So, therefore, what is wrong with some of us?

Mark, chapter 11, they were looking only for a national leader rather than a Spiritual Savior. Greed is also believing that what was received is not what you desired; greed then dictates that you dispose of what you perceive as no good to you (*excess beyond its needs*). He is all they needed, but not as they saw it. How do you see Him? Are you who you thought you were?

Those who claim to be in tune with God and do not abide in His Word are the greediest of all; keep in mind that greed is not just about wealth, but also power and status. The Pharisees and Sadducees boldly held to this claim. *Power is not a bad thing and is not difficult to handle; all one has to do is know how to use it.* They were leaning towards their wisdom. Many others hold on to a different claim; they desire to be rich and powerful, just as the rich of this world, who have given power over them because they are rich (*only God can give true power, not the world*). They attempt to justify their greed with a scripture or two, such as *John 14:13 KJV;* And *whatsoever ye shall ask in my name, that will I do*, that the Father may be glorified in the Son, or *Psalm 37:4 KJV*, "Delight yourself in the Lord and *he will give you the desires of your heart.*" Those desires should be God-glorifying; when our desires are felt as a means to a God-centered end, this will always give God the glory. The desires of our hearts should be, concerning God's kingdom and God's will (*this will keep you from giving in to greed*), not a private jet, unless that jet is a means to get you to and fro on a mission that God specifically put you on a path to. Just in case you did not know, those two scriptures are based on a condition found in *the following scriptures: John 15:7 KJV: If ye abide in me, and my words abide in you, ye shall ask what ye will, and it shall be done unto you. Hebrews 13:5 KJV Keep your life free from the love of money, and be content with what you have,* for he has said, "I will never leave you nor forsake you." *1 John 5:14 KJV*, "This is the confidence which we have before him, that, if we ask anything *according to his will*, he hears us."

And He said to them, "Take care, and be on your guard against all covetousness, for one's life does not consist in the abundance of his possessions", *Luke 12:15 KJV*. Sometimes, the abundance of possessions, or the lack thereof, causes us to turn our focus towards those things; the abundance tends to make us feel somewhat powerful, but not powerful in the right context; the power we should feel; is that we now have the power to help someone in need of what we possess; believing God gave it to you for that reason, knowing that you would not allow greed to overtake your desire to do His will. The lack of abundance shifts our focus on self as well, for we now cry, "Woe is me, oh Lord", why must I suffer this lack of possessions? Did you ever think it might be because you permit greed to override your desire to do God's will? Are you who you thought you were? *Proverbs 11:24 KJV* says, "one gives freely, yet grows all the richer; another withholds what he should give, and only suffers want".

"For everything in the world—the lust of the flesh, the lust of the eyes, and the pride of life—comes not from the Father but from the world", *1 John 2:16 NIV*. "We know that we have passed from death to life because we love the brethren. He who does not love *his* brother abides in death", *1 John 3:14 NKJV*.

2 Samuel 11 David was overtaken by greed; God was displeased, but God did not punish David for what he did concerning Bathsheba. David's sin is what punished him. Sin has a long-lasting effect; this is why God tells us to practice righteousness (*The end preexists in the means*). Out of his sin came adultery and murder; out of those came the death of their child, the loss of respect, and the memory of the guilt which we see in *Psalms 51*. These things would not have come from a righteous act.

Ephesians 5 and Colossians 3 pronounced greed as idolatry. There are expressions of greed practiced, but not boldly pronounced: satan blindsided you, now you're always seeking more ways to make more money; feeling good and finding relief in shopping (*shopping for someone else would not be considered, unless; you are doing it for recognition*); You hate paying taxes while giving honor to those who find way to avoid paying taxes; you want to do it also, you know, not pay taxes; *but first consider the consequences.* You feel somewhat imposed upon when your children ask you for money for what they need; your greed did not allow you to see their need; they had to ask. God has a solution for greed: Grow into the character of God by faith; God's character involves contentment; God lacks nothing and wants nothing;

be content in whatever circumstance you find yourself in until you hear from God; the abundance of Christ's life is to be enough. Greed is contrary to God's character. Greed is personal aspirations; seeking only for oneself. When your focus is on things of this world (*materialism*), living for possessions, your desire to be like Christ is replaced by expressions of greed, which becomes an act of greed when your focus shifts to actions. Greed replaces strength, making individuals vulnerable to get-rich-quick schemes; receiving desired things (*not necessarily money*) for unmentionable acts; and conducting shady business (offering people no good goods, Amos 8:5). "Nothing makes us more vulnerable than loneliness, except greed", *Thomas Harris.*

Greed is to keep it for oneself, far beyond the dictates of basic survival and comfort.

Here comes the fight: Greed weighs heavily in places of worship; what started as a movement led by God established a place of worship, but somewhere along the way, God's instructions were not followed as given, overshadowed by greed. God does not fail; man does when he stops listening to God. *Perception is not always the reality; Are you who you thought you were?* History validates this claim with many Old Testament great kings, even Solomon, who gave in to avarice, cupidity, or covetousness. All of the worship buildings today were not built to please God; some were to please man, a way to wow the people; feeding on the desires of people who love the latest and the greatest thing; those who like to flock to whatever is new, not to seek God. Deception is the gospel preached: give us all your money to care for God's house; don't worry about your affairs; God will bless you, etc; sacrifice large amounts of money, to show God your faithfulness; leaders allow you to see them giving large amounts of money, then ask you to sacrifice with them, but they get theirs back after it's all said and done. The expressions of greed involve: always pronouncing that you have over 2000 members, etc.; all the great work being done in the community that you are paying for, not your tithes and free will offerings; you are always being asked for more money above tithes and free will offerings; pledging more to support the everyday expenses of the worship place."Every great cause begins as a movement, becomes a business, and eventually degenerates into a racket." *Eric Hoffer.* "Knowledge is: knowing a tomato is a fruit. Wisdom is not putting it in a fruit salad," *Miles Kingston.*

God never intended for us to *worship the idea* of having more than what we need; Jesus came in humility, not glory; Jesus' message was for us to seek the kingdom of God first. "The Bible does not say money is the root of all evil; it says the *love of money* is the root of all kinds of evil. A poor man who, in his heart, worships the idea of being rich is more vulnerable to its evils than a rich man who has a heart to use it all for the Lord", *Criss Jami.*

"We always want what is not ours. It's intriguing. We think if we can just get that, we'll finally be happy. The lure of what we do not have is deceptive. True freedom, however, is found in being content with what we already have. Can you imagine it? Can you imagine being whole, complete, fulfilled, and content with what you already have? It sounds too good to be true. Utter satisfaction? That is freedom. That is what everyone is searching for. Where, though, can you find this kind of contentment? I've noticed that the more I've come to know Jesus, the less I've desired material things. Materialism is what happens when you find your joy in things. Contentment is what happens when you find your joy in Jesus. They're complete opposites. You can easily differentiate a materialistic person from a content person", *Cole Ryan.* When Jesus said "seek ye first the kingdom of heaven" (*Matthew 6:33*), He was telling us to focus on seeking His salvation, living in obedience to Him, and sharing the good news of the kingdom with others so that they might obtain what we have, in return, He will take care of our business as He promised.

The poor worry about what they don't have; the rich worry about retaining what they have. In a sense, the poor and the rich are on the same page: the poor are concerned about becoming poorer; the rich are also concerned about avoiding becoming poor. Contentment is learned from experiencing both abundance and the lack thereof (*Philippians 4:12*). Sometimes, a time of poverty is what is needed; remember, all He does is for your good. God is our shepherd; He is more than enough, that we should not want another. He causes us to lie down in green pastures when He deems it necessary: He leadeth us beside the still waters. He gives us rest in Him when we need it, He calms us, freeing us from the worries of the world. *Job 1-2* tells how God restores us, and *1 Kings 18-19* tells the same. They tell how, after a time of loss and solitude, God restores. He restoreth my soul: he leadeth me in the paths of righteousness for his name's sake, not any other, that He may get the glory, not another. After the experience of Job and Elijah, surely, God got the glory. Theirs was not about materialism but about contentment in the promise of God.

A dog was previously used as an example of greed, but a dog can also be used as an example of contentment. When a dog is with its beloved master, no matter what happens, it remains content. For example, if it is raining, and the dog is outside alone, it will run for cover and desire to be inside with its master. Now, if the master is standing in the rain with the dog, the dog is content to be wherever its master is, and the rain is no longer a concern. Not to call anybody a dog, but isn't this what Jesus was saying? If we focus on being true to Him and desire to be where He is, then the cares of this world will fade away. *Are you who you thought you were?*

Cupidity can also be described as having a continuous need to receive from others (*some people are worthless without others' approval*). An attempt to show charity to another without knowing what God would have us to do, not knowing what they truly need, giving them a greater desire to depend on us. This type of action injures more than it heals unless we know what they truly need. To give a "wine-o" wine does not help; to give a man you believe is cold, a coat is injurious if it is food that he needs. All some need is a word from God. First, pray that the word be delivered clearly, and that the understanding thereof is received. That word might be to encourage independence, rather than dependence. All that appears to need a helping hand is not always as they appear because p*erception is not always reality.* "Charity is injurious unless it helps the recipient to become independent of it", *John D. Rockefeller.* Awareness is the key to the truth, and the truth will set your mind free.

Chapter 10

Deception
*("O, what a tangled web we weave when
first we practice to deceive!" Sir Walter Scott)*

The idea of Santa Claus, the Tooth Fairy, the Easter Bunny, Easter eggs, and other methods parents use to deceive their children are all tricks of the devil. satan is the father of lies and deception; his methods are subtle, leading you away from the truth before you are exposed to the truth. When the truth of these things is discovered, they can lead one to be suspicious of the truth when it is later presented. "Adults find pleasure in deceiving a child. They consider it necessary, but they also enjoy it. The children very quickly figure it out and then practice deception themselves", *Elias Canetti.*

"Obedience opens the door to the constant companionship of the Holy Ghost. And the spiritual gifts and abilities activated by the power of the Holy Ghost enable us to avoid deception and to see, to feel, to know, to understand, and to remember things as they really are", *David Bednar.* In the book of *Esther*, we see that Haman was hanged on the gallows that he had prepared for Mordecai. Haman occupied a high position given to him by King Ahasuerus. Haman had a seat above all the princes that were with him. And all the king's servants that were in the king's gate, bowed, and reverenced Haman: for the king had so commanded concerning him. But Mordecai bowed not, nor did he reverence. This rubbed Haman a bit raw; he was angry and developed a strong dislike for Mordecai. Later in the story, Haman was deceived by his wife and friends; he built a gallows to hang Mordecai, but in the end, it was he who was hanged on the gallows that he built for Mordecai. "The greatest deception men suffer is from their own opinions," *Leonardo da Vinci. Proverbs 3* warns us of this.

We must learn to practice truth once it is discovered. satan wants us to be skeptical of what is true, leading us to believe that lies and deception are the truth. He uses things that are common to you; things that you find pleasure in doing; Santa Claus, the Tooth Fairy, the Easter Bunny, and Halloween; but if it were not so, we would not find pleasure in pacifying our children with these lies. Some are so excited about deceiving their children that they can't wait until Christmas and Easter; they prepare for these events to deceive their children again and again. Dad (*the head of the household; the leader God set forth to lead his family into righteousness*) dresses up as Santa to deceive his children. Mom gets excited about Easter; they decorate with eggs and rabbits, and dress up the kids to go to church to hear the real truth, but yet, continue the lie when they get home with the Easter egg hunt. To the children, it's all about that. "Worse than telling a lie is spending your whole life staying true to a lie", *Robert Brault.*

"If you want to become fully mature in the Lord, you must learn to love truth. Otherwise, you will always leave open a door of deception for the enemy to take what is meant to be yours", *Joyce Meyer.* But be ye doers of the word, and not hearers only, deceiving your own selves. *James 1:22 KJV.* The truth that is preached on these special days, or should be preached on Christmas and Easter, if presented correctly, should show how the word of God can be a wall, a shield, a form of protection against deception. "Knowledge of God's Word is a bulwark against deception, temptation, accusation, even persecution", *Edwin*

Louis Cole. "Lying lips *are* an abomination to the LORD: but they that deal truly *are* his delight", *Proverbs 12:22 KJV.*

Let us look at "the season to be jolly" for a moment; Christmas time is when we feel pressured to buy merchandise for others, which can lead to disappointment when the thoughtfulness is not reciprocated. Is that what God, who commands us to love one another, would want? Who benefits the most from this season? (*Hosea 12:7*) Keep in mind that this season does not bring jolliness to all; some become depressed and sad, and other negative emotions because they don't have it to give; they can't keep up with the Joneses. These are the ones wise enough to know their state; they can't afford to engage in jolly giving. Others are not so wise; they borrow money (*credit cards, store revolving accounts*) and they enter into debt, far beyond their means. Does this honor God? What honors God is: the love we have for Him and one another all year, not just at the end, *just a note*. Remember, satan wants us to be skeptical of what is true, leading us to believe that his lies and deception are the truth. I know some of you are saying, "We donate to charities and other entities to help people in need; much is collected and distributed this time of the year to bring joy to those sad hearts." My question is, don't they need it before this time of year? Are you there yet?

To guard against these types of deception, we must follow what *Roman 12:2 KJV* says: "And be not conformed to this world: but be ye transformed by the renewing of your mind, that ye may prove, what *is* that good, and acceptable, and perfect, will of God". If we continue to deceive the children, the future generations, we will be teaching them deception rather than truth. This is satan's aim: to deceive the world; those who don't believe have disbelief because they have become skeptics due to the lies they were taught as children, by the ones they trusted for the truth; *the end preexists in the means*. It is what it is. This is why you have people not committed to the way of Christ; not seeking the greatest good of another (*for He said that you will know they are mine by the love they have, one for another*); doing all things that please them rather than God; conforming to the way of the world; advocating lawlessness (*2 Timothy3:2*), but yet, stand in front of a crowd and say:" first I want to thank God, who is the head of my life", but it is not God who they follow. This is not to be taken as judgment, but just trying the spirit by the spirit. The word says what it says. *"This* I say then, Walk in the Spirit, and ye shall not fulfill the lust of the flesh", *Galatians 5:16 KJV.* We also appease our children by allowing them to choose what and who they listen to, meaning you don't know what or who they are listening to; you are not certain of the messages in the music they worship. If you have not filled them with truth, they have no armor against the weapons of our enemy. "To the man who only has a hammer, everything he encounters begins to look like a nail," *Abraham Maslow.* "The integrity of the upright shall guide them: but the perverseness of transgressors shall destroy them" *Proverbs 11:3 KJV.*

satan has deceived in so many ways it is hard to keep count; he has even deceived some in their fasting. This is why some tell everybody that they are fasting. Fasting is letting go of the passions of the flesh for a time of repentance and heartfelt prayer because what is going on in the heart is important to God. To gain mastery over oneself and to conquer the passions of the flesh is the purpose of fasting. God wants our desire to be a need to liberate ourselves from dependence on the things of this world and shift our focus to the things of the Kingdom of God. Scripture teaches that some forms of evil cannot be conquered without it (*Matthew 17:15-21, Mark 9:23-29*). The end preexists in the means. Hypocritical fasting is wrong; others are not to be aware of it. Fasting endured for public praise is the deception of satan. *Matthew 6: 16-18*

Man tends to think of himself as the guy who knows, "The Barber Shop Prophet", the man who has it going on. He believes he can solve deep mysteries; he believes himself to be wiser than his audience. The wisdom they have is of no value but to themselves (For if a man thinks himself to be something, when he is nothing, he deceiveth himself, Galatians 6). But, in all his knowledge, he didn't know that the greatest form of deception is when men masquerade as the head of the family, and they are everything but. The wife practices deception and brags about it to her girlfriends, telling them how she lets him think he is running things at home; he is being manipulated and doesn't know it. The man allows outsiders to manipulate his household, mainly by allowing others to manipulate the wife's way of thinking. A true head of the house is to educate the family on the things of God; he can't teach what he doesn't know. *First*: He must obtain the peace of God before considering becoming the head of the house. To be a true head of the family, one must know God to know His ways. *Second*: He must keep everybody else out of their private business; this is done by educating the family in such a manner. What happens behind closed doors should stay behind closed doors. In other words, nobody needs to know what was argued about last night except those involved; none of the girlfriends or the guys, because they will have opinions that only may work for them, not you and yours. Now, because God has laid down the plan and how things should go, if we live and love according to His word; this does not mean that if the head is abusing the rest of the family; because that is not following God; that requires outside intervention after much prayer, but only to be shared with whom the spirit of God direct to intervene. *Third*: The head needs to learn to avoid stress, anxiety, and chaos and lead the family away from these destructive elements. When the head is weak, the family suffers; there is no oneness of minds; a lot of division, and we know the saying: *"Together we stand, divided we fall" unknown*. "Jesus knew their thoughts and said to them, "Every kingdom divided against itself will be ruined, and every city or household divided against itself will not stand", *Matthew 12:25 NIV*.

Genesis chapters 25-30 show us deception in the family. Rebekah helped Jacob deceive Isaac; Jacob was deceived by his uncle Laban; one deception after another. "Adults find pleasure in deceiving a child. They consider it necessary, but they also enjoy it. The children very quickly figure it out and then practice deception themselves", *Elias*

Canetti. God was aware of these deceptive actions, but He did not sanction them; He used them as a means to His end. Remember, *the end preexists in the means.* Even though they were tangled in the web of deception, God still used it for good.

"Whenever, therefore, people are deceived and form opinions wide of the truth, it is clear that the error has slid into their minds through the medium of certain resemblances to that truth", *Socrates*. Therefore, in closing, deception is a battle that affects persuasion; to persuade, the responsible cause of the differences that exist in each of us has to be known first. It has to enumerate all causes that act and necessitate a particular type of persuasion for each of those differences. Deception is only effective when individual souls need to follow that type of persuasion. Some are easily persuaded by certain forms of persuasion, while others of different character are not so easily affected by the same persuasion. These distinctions need to be completely understood by the deceiver for the persuasion to take effect. Remember, satan is the master deceiver; the father of all that is opposite of truth. Thank God we have the Holy Spirit to guide us through this process; we would still be unbelievers, allowing satan's persuasion to deceive us. When the Holy Spirit directs you to do the opposite of what you were thinking of doing, and you do that anyway, then it's on you. "Be not deceived; God is not mocked: for whatsoever a man soweth, that shall he also reap" *Galatians 6:7-15 KJV*. The kingdom is an established rule of God's government. Christians have been transferred from the kingdom of darkness to the kingdom of light (God's rule). God's kingdom has an order of rule, the way things flow. The kingdom of darkness wants to impose its rule within the kingdom of God so that it will not function as God intended.

To spot deception, you must first be shown what deception is. The Holy Spirit shows you deception in its fullness, so that you know [Identify] what is so that you may speak truth to those who are deceived. Whatever the opposition offers you that sounds like what you need is for their benefit, not yours; the oppositionists don't care about you. The deceiver: only wants you to help them tear down whatever God has built, creating chaos they control. Then come to the rescue on the white horse to solve problems they created; now they look like the savior.

Chapter 11

Hurry up and wait
(*The Tortoise & the Hare*)

    This chapter is about overconfidence in our ability and our impatience. The Bible states: "I returned, and saw under the sun, that the race is not to the swift, nor the battle to the strong, neither yet bread to the wise, nor yet riches to men of understanding, nor yet favour to men of skill; but time and chance happeneth to them all." *Ecclesiastes l 9:11 KJV*. In this, we want to point out that overconfidence sometimes causes us to hurry up and wait.

    We often see people who remind us of this story; they seem to be in a hurry, always. Some do not know where they are going, but they are in a hurry to get there (*"I don't know where I'm going, but I'm on my way"*). Here's an example: A slow but careful person (*the Tortoise*) pulls into a store parking lot, and a car comes behind them (*"the Hare"*), speeding as if they are in a big hurry. This vehicle flies past the *Tortoise* and parks, but the *Tortoise*, as slow as they are (*according to the Hare*), finally gets to a parking spot, discovering the speedster "*Hare*" has not exited their vehicle yet (*"but they were in a rush"*). Their delay is because their overconfidence in their speed has caused them to overlook something; they are still looking for something in their vehicle that they need in the store (*just as the Hare was when his confidence in being ahead caused him to nap)*. The *Tortoise* goes into the store, gets what they need, and leaves. The *Tortoise* eventually wins, even though it was not racing to win. I imagine the *Hare* in the store taking their time, but when they reach the checkout, they are in a hurry again. "Why aren't more checkout lanes open"? They ask. "Can we get another checker"? They are in a state of Hurry up and wait. The best example of all is church folk. People rush to end church service to spend an hour in the parking lot talking before they go home. What was the big rush? There are many more I could give, but I'm only going to give one more. The *Tortoise* is driving down the road; a red light is visible in the distance. The hare came flying past the *Tortoise*, not realizing that it was only to hurry up and wait, because they got there first, they had to stop at the red light, by the time the *Tortoise* got there the light had turned green and never had to stop but pass the *Hare* by because; the car in front of the *Hare* had no idea the light had turned green. Again, patience has caused the *Tortoise* to win a race that was not a race; the *Hare*, again, has put himself in a state of "hurry up and wait". Now, if you were the Hare, then you are not who you thought you were.

Being patient will get you what you desire, without wanting it so that you become impatient while waiting. Patience comes from knowing the value of what you are waiting for.

"Patience is not simply the ability to wait – it is how we behave; while we're waiting", *Joyce Meyer*. Most commonly, people are in a hurry to obtain as much as they can, rather than receiving what is at hand. When greed overtakes you, common sense and patience take a back seat, and thoughtlessness sets in. Your wisdom can't function because greed blocks its path from the wisdom of God. If there was a stack of money on the ground, banded together, as you approached, the band broke, and the money started to blow in the wind. Most would begin to snatch as much from the air as possible to avoid it getting away. Greed takes over at this point, and your focus is not on what is, but what could be. While you are chasing what is in the air, you are getting further away from that which you could have obtained; the money on the ground at hand, but you wanted all of it (*greed*), not just some, not realizing that it wasn't yours anyway, and any amount gained is more than what you had before you saw it. You probably will never know if those were dollars in the air and hundreds on the ground because you were blinded by the rush (*greed*) and that was your focus. Never was it mentioned that someone other than you was at this place; there was no need to rush to collect the money; confidence causes us to arrive at the point that God would have us arrive too soon; this can cause us to wander and nap, like the Hare. Getting there when God planned for you to be there (Tortoise), all that was in the air would have landed by now, and you could have it all. While the Hare was napping, the Tortoise was collecting the money from the air that the Hare missed, which is now on the ground. "The man that wandereth out of the way of understanding shall remain in the congregation of the dead" *Proverbs 21:16 KJV*.

For years, certain people have tried to separate themselves from all that is not like them. They are *quick* to separate, but *slow* to band together until there is trouble; they desire to band together and say "we are one". The same people appear to be committed to the pledge of allegiance, but not all of it. The word that stands out is "indivisible"; unable to be divided. Some have allowed one man to promote division in every word he speaks. That part about liberty, and justice for all, they forget, until trouble arises, then "we are one" finds its way back. This is why the greedy (*overconfident*) and the envious are *slow* to achieve eternal things, but *fast* at achieving temporal things; the banding together is only for their sake, not for the sake of all. The race is not to the swift' (*Ecclesiastes 9:11 KJV*). "The key to everything is patience. You get the chicken by hatching the egg, not by smashing it", *Arnold H. Glasow.*

It was not the Tortoise's conduct in taking on a bully that was emphasized, but the Hare's foolish overconfidence. "Many people have good natural abilities which are ruined by idleness; on the other hand, sobriety, zeal, and perseverance can prevail over indolence", *Unknown*. These examples are to bring awareness. Awareness is the key to the truth, and the truth will set your mind free. Now, there is an alternate version of this story. In this version, the hare realized the stupidity of the race and gave up. This is still overconfidence because the hare assumed he would win because of his speed. At the end of this version, fire erupted in the forest, but not all of the forest beasts survived. They called a quick meeting to decide what messenger to send with a warning for the beasts in the forest; they sent the Tortoise. Swiftness has its place. "The difference between 'try' and 'triumph' is just a little umph", *Bonnie Przybylski*.

12 Chapter

Selfishness

(I'm Just Doing Me)

We are selfish by nature. To be unselfish (*humility*), we have to learn that. *Genesis 4:9*, the question was asked: "Am I my brother's keeper?" After this chapter, maybe you can answer that on your own. Imagine a person parking in a public spot, taking up two spaces to protect their vehicle, or maybe just because of the thoughtlessness of others; maybe it was done because of selfishness. As we discussed in the chapter on cause and effect, this affects the whole, not just that person; this is a selfish act, and that's the truth.

Imagine a person in a line at the grocery store, their basket is overflowing (*they are blessed and don't acknowledge it*), someone walks up with one or two items; there are no express lanes open, due to thoughtlessness; since thoughtlessness voids awareness of anyone's needs other than your own; the offer to let that person go ahead of them is never offered; you would think, being blessed in such a way to have groceries overflowing in their cart; thankfulness would bring about considering others needs before their own would be at the top of the list. Not! Selfishness knows no others. That's the truth; thoughtlessness voids awareness. This is another of satan's subtle ways of deception. Selfishness is why satan is a fallen angel. The idea of selfishness is me, me, me; mine, mine, mine (*pride*), but it is destructive. Selfishness destroys your character, and when you get that haunting spirit, you know, "if I go down, I'm taking somebody with me", which indicates that you know you are falling. "Pride goeth before destruction, and a haughty spirit before a fall", *Proverbs 16:18 KJV.*

Imagine a person at home all day, with only one thing to accomplish that day; waiting almost until the close of business to do it, to avoid having to wait in a line (*selfishness*) or be inconvenienced by their time. Well, this action just inconvenienced the time of another; the employees of that business who had to serve you at closing. What you need takes time; time is not plentiful at this hour. If this business refuses, you say, "That's not right, and it's not my fault". Is it? This business has to extend work hours just for you; Remember, cause and effect. You figure out the details, but this is a selfish act, and that's the truth; most don't see this until they are on the wrong end of it, you know, working at that place when someone comes in at the last minute, and you call them everything but a child of God. *John Chapter 5 KJV* tells the story of a man who, for 38 years, suffered an infirmity; he couldn't get someone to help him in the pool of Bethesda to get healed. *Verse 7* "The impotent man answered him, Sir, I have no man, when the water is troubled, to put me into the pool: but while I am coming, another steppeth down before me." This is selfishness at best. In *verse 6,* "When Jesus saw him lie, and knew that he had been now a long time in that case, he saith unto him, Wilt thou be made whole?", I have to assume, somebody else knew he had been there a long while also, but thoughtlessness voids awareness. Imagine being in traffic, and the line is moving very slowly; here comes someone driving to the front of that line, which you have been in for a while now; they want you to let them in because they don't want to wait in line as you did, and will get angry if you don't. For whatever reason, whether they didn't want to wait in line or just decided at the last minute that they wanted to go that way, it is a selfish act on their part to expect you to sacrifice for them when they gave your position no thought at all. This has nothing to do with you not exercising love; this is not a need for them; it is a selfish want. That individual had the same opportunity as you, in the same line; they just wanted to be at the front. This is selfishness. *Philippians 2 KJV* tells us what we should liken ourselves to, and how it relates to selfishness. Emphasis on *verse 4*: "Look not every man on his own things, but every man *also* on the things of *others*". People that satan has blinded with their ambitions are generally those who desire to be great down here, but not great in God's eyes.

1 Corinthians 13 4-7 states; Love suffereth long, and is kind; love envieth not; love vaunteth not itself, is not puffed up, Doth not behave itself unseemly, seeketh not her own, is not easily provoked, thinketh no evil; Rejoiceth not in iniquity, but rejoiceth in the truth; Beareth all things, believeth all things, hopeth all things, endureth all things. Does any of these sound like selfishness? But you must keep in mind that all of these are choices.

Selfishness dictates that some should be forced or compelled to handouts, and should not be allowed the same opportunities as others because they are different, they are not like the majority. The truth is that all should be allowed to showcase and honor God through the talents He has placed in their care. Imagine this: there are two ladders and two people; if there is a prize at the top, whoever reaches the top first wins. They both had an equal opportunity to afford the same thing; no special treatment; no handouts; no feeling sorry for one another; having pity, just an equal chance at an opportunity for the same thing, and the best won. That is an unselfish act!

Blessed are the poor in spirit (*humble*), Blessed are the meek (*longsuffering & patient*), Blessed are the merciful (*mercy shown is mercy received*), Blessed are the pure in heart (*people of integrity*), Blessed are the peacemakers (*people loving others as themselves*), *Matthew 5:1-12*. We cannot credit God as Daniel did (*Daniel 2, when he interpreted the king's dream*) with a selfish attitude; Daniel was unselfish (*humble*).

"The heavens declare the glory of God; and the firmament shows His handiwork", *Psalm 19:1 KJV.* "Since the creation of the world His invisible attributes are clearly seen", *Romans 1:20 KJV.* God made us as He did, and that's it: no mistakes; how we look is no accident, not meant for you to change the way you look. From observing nature, it is hard to believe God does not exist and has power, intelligence, and a flair for beauty! Selfishness dictates that we alter our appearance to satisfy our ego or to please another who dislikes what God has done and probably won't like it after the alteration. If we *believe* in God and *that* all *He* does *is* for our good, and that *He rewards* our faithfulness, however, our faithfulness only comes if we believe. Belief leads us to *seek Him diligently (Heb 11:6 KJV).* The difference in our appearance is for our sake, not His. When we learn to look past those things (*selfishness*), we arrive at the place that He intended for us to be. If we are so concerned with public opinion, why not desire an opinion of integrity? To be in the public eye only to promote your selfishness is vanity. If you were raised without love (*allowed to do whatever you wanted without any discipline at home*), all you promote is **"just do you"**, then all you are doing is corrupting those who see you as an idol. Since they idolize you, teach them discipline, even though you were raised at home without it; you did receive it at some point in your early life, and it did prove to have a positive influence. If you help just one person avoid the pitfalls you faced, then you have done a world of good by showing what love is. Awareness is the key to the truth, and the truth will set your mind free.

Jesus reminds His disciples, in the Beatitudes, that they cannot seek happiness the way the world does. He was teaching them that they cannot find true joy with selfish ambition, self-justification, or excuses. A state of blessedness comes to those who mourn over their sin. "These are the ones I look on with favor: those who are humble and contrite in spirit, and who tremble at my word" (*Isaiah 66:2 KJV*).

The term *mourn* means "to experience deep grief." In His teaching on spiritual blessedness, Jesus seems to indicate that this mourning is

NO REFLECTION, ARE YOU WHO YOU THOUGHT YOU WERE?
87

due to grief over sin. People who agree with God about the evil of their hearts can achieve a state of blessedness because of the comfort they receive from communion with the Holy Spirit. Jesus called the Holy Spirit the Comforter *(John 14:16, 26; 15:26; 2 Corinthians 1:4)*. The Holy Spirit comforts those who are honest about their sin and *humble enough* to ask for forgiveness and healing. Those who hide their sin or try to justify it can never know the comfort that comes from a pure heart, as Jesus talks about in *Matthew 5:8 (Proverbs 28:13; Isaiah 57:15)*. The kind of "mourning" that leads to repentance is truly blessed *(2 Corinthians 7:10)*. Some people will accuse you of being who they are while excluding themselves. Let me explain. You are seated at the movie theater, hoping for a peaceful night; here come the uncivilized; they have no deep grief concerning their sins because, as far as they are concerned, they don't have any. They come in talking loudly, disturbing everyone else, and when someone asks them to be a little quieter, they say to one of their party members: *"Girl, I can't stand to be around ignorant folk; please deliver me from them God"*. They are talking about you, charging you with the wrong they committed. Amazing, isn't it? You can't grow apples by planting watermelon seeds; *the end preexists in the means.* These do not agree with God about the evils in their hearts. satan has deceived them into thinking that all is wrong but them. "Our attitude towards others determines their attitude towards us", *Earl Nightingale.*

"For the *love of money* is the root of all evil: which while some coveted after, they have erred from the faith, and pierced themselves through with many sorrows", *1 Timothy 6:10 KJV*. To desire wealth for personal satisfaction is selfish; to desire wealth to help someone or support a cause that helps the less fortunate is selflessness *(humility)*. How many people desire wealth for reasons other than their satisfaction? "But they that will be rich fall into temptation and a snare, and into many foolish and hurtful lusts, which drown men in destruction and perdition", *1Timothy 6:9 KJV*. Some who have obtained wealth believe they do not need to ask God for anything; they can provide for themselves. They raise themselves above all others because of their wealth.

When selflessness comes into play, we agree with *Timothy 6:17-18 KJV* "Charge them that are rich in this world, that they be not highminded, nor trust in uncertain riches, but in the living God, who giveth us richly all things to enjoy;" "That they do good, that they be rich in good works, ready to distribute, willing to communicate." When wealth changes our character, we become like a fast driver who drives too fast to see the sign that reads: "The road ahead is closed because the bridge has fallen into the river". Awareness is the key to the truth, and the truth will set your mind free. "If selfishness is the key to being miserable, then selflessness must be the key to being happy!" *Joyce Meyer.*

13 Chapter

Trust in God's plan
"But without faith it is impossible to [walk with God and] please Him, for whoever comes [near] to God must [necessarily] believe that God exists and that He rewards those who [earnestly and diligently] seek Him", Hebrews 11:6 AMP.

I know you have heard about your foundation being on rocks or sand, something to that effect. Well, here is my take on that: If you live in the state of Texas, especially the mid to southern parts, then you know what happens to what you thought was a solid foundation. It is only as good as the soil it rests upon. In Texas, the soil shifts from season to season, causing your foundation to shift, and you start noticing cracks in walls and doors with gaps, etc. Other states have better soil and no foundation issues, at least, not to the magnitude we experience in Texas. Life's foundation is the same in a sense; the state you are in determines the magnitude of the issues with your foundation.

A foundation in a state of condemnation and despair is like a slab foundation in Texas, where clay soil shrinks and expands, causing instability, yielding cracks in walls, gaps in doors, houses leaning in one direction, etc. In life, this foundation yields depravity, which in turn yields anxiety, which leads to broken hearts, depression, sadness, and fear. All of which can come from being different from the majority. Remember, anxiety is the paranoia of something out there that seems menacing but may not be frightening, and, indeed, may not even be out there. "Neither comprehension nor learning can take place in an atmosphere of anxiety", *Rose Kennedy.*

These emotions might be someone struggling with alcoholism, drug addiction, confusion about sexual orientation, etc. You have struggled with these things for a long time, going from victory to defeat. Jesus said: "Come unto me, all ye that labour and are heavy laden, and I will give you rest. Take my yoke upon you, and learn of me; for I am meek and lowly in heart: and ye shall find rest unto your souls. For my yoke is easy, and my burden is light." (*Matthew 11:28–30 KJV*)

The foundation of Jesus Christ (*the state of resting on the Word of God*) is like the other states that do not have this issue with the clay soil. It rests on what Jesus did on the cross at Calvary; that is where redemption comes from. The Bible tells us that a war is raging in our hearts that will not rest until we see Him face to face (*Galatians 5:16–17 KJV*). This is why we must trust in His plan.

In Colossians 4, Paul tells them to devote themselves to prayer; he told them to pray that God would open doors for the message; he told them to pray that it may be delivered clearly; he also told them to let their conversation be always full of grace, seasoned with salt, so that they may know how to answer everyone. This still needs to be done today to get others to trust in God's plan.

"Encouragement is one of the most powerful ministries on earth."

The unbeliever will attempt to deceive you in matters most common to you, for example; "if God loves you so much; why does He allow you to struggle so much ?" or "If God loves you so much; why did He allow the tornado to destroy your house?" or Why did God take your child at such a young age?" We don't always know the answers to these questions that one might seek, but we do know we must trust in His plan. Whatever God allows, we must never forget that all He does

NO REFLECTION, ARE YOU WHO YOU THOUGHT YOU WERE?

is for our good; we might not see it in the storm, but, after the storm, it starts to come together. Yes, it is easier said than done, but the more you practice, the better you become. The deceiver will have you believe you are being punished by the God who says He loves you. These things are not necessarily punishment for you, but part of a bigger plan that is a means to an end. Remember, whatsoever a man soweth, that he shall also reap and only that. To be clear, it is your sins that punish you (*the end preexists in the means)*; this is why God warned you of the consequences that come after. He is only seeking your greatest good. Everything God warned you not to do was not as the deceiver would have you believe (*denying you pleasure*), but to keep you from punishment.

"We all know that light travels faster than sound. That's why certain people appear bright until you hear them speak." *Albert Einstein. 1 Tim 6:3-4* If anyone advocates a different doctrine that does not agree with sound words, those of our Lord Jesus Christ, and with the doctrine conforming to godliness, he is conceited and understands nothing; but, he has a morbid interest in controversial questions and disputes about words, out of which arise envy, strife, abusive language, evil suspicions". The Saturday morning 'Barber Shop Prophet' is usually influenced by satan himself, if his words are confrontational. *2 Thessalonians 2* speaks of the coming of our Lord Jesus Christ and how we are not to allow deception to keep us from holding fast to the truth. We must trust in God's plan and not conform to the way of the unbeliever, which is: the word of God contradicts itself. "Contradictions do not exist. Whenever you think you are facing a contradiction, check your premises. You will find that one of them is wrong", *Ayn Rand*.

The deceiver will also attempt to lead you into believing that God needs no help, and since God needs no help, Jesus was just a good man, another prophet, not God's only begotten Son. He is no different from John, Matthew, Peter, or Paul. To go further, he will also have you believe that the only important books of the Bible are the Old Testament books, and even further, just the first five.

"What was silent in the father speaks in the Son, and often I found in the son the unveiled secret of the father," *Friedrich Nietzsche*. Truth: God is more than we can bear; He had to veil Himself in Jesus for us to see Him at all, but, as you can see, even Jesus was too much; that is why the deceiver wants you to believe He was not who He claimed to be. God loves us so much; He wants us to know Him. "One of the deep secrets of life is that all that is really worth doing is what we do for others", *Lewis Carroll*.

The deceiver has diluted the thinking of many; there have been wars for the sake of religion; races that don't like another race, because of the deceiver who has tricked them into hate. As long as there is hate for another, the deceiver has a foothold. "I refuse to accept the view that mankind is so tragically bound to the starless midnight of racism and war that the bright daybreak of peace and brotherhood can never become a reality... I believe that unarmed truth and unconditional love will have the final word", *Martin Luther King, Jr.* Trust in God's Plan. "Rivers, ponds, lakes, and streams; they all have different names, but all contain water. Just as religions do, they all contain truths." *Muhammad Ali*. The deceiver keeps you focused on religion, and this is what all the disagreements are about. God never told you to focus on religion; He only wants us to trust in His plan, that is, trust that He knows what is best for us. Religion could be anything, worshiping snakes, rats, birds, etc. "Nothing in the world is more dangerous than sincere ignorance and conscientious stupidity," *Martin Luther King, Jr.* According to some, religion has values, since there is some truth to most religions. It's just that somewhere they differ, and therein lies the problem; disagreements have begun wars. This quote was just too humorous to leave out. "Religion is what keeps the poor from murdering the rich", *Napoleon Bonaparte*.

God's Plan is for us to love one another as He loves us. Love is a mighty weapon against principalities in high places. The deceiver plans to keep you from loving one another and fighting him; for those who love to fight; to others, he claims, not to exist; he knows you can't win without love; God is love. "It is wonderful how much time good people spend fighting the devil. If they would only expend the same amount of energy loving their fellow men, the devil would die in his own tracks of ennui", *Helen Keller*. Before you prepare for your next fight with the devil, consider this: the main event is not your fight with satan, but resisting him much harder than that; resisting him requires more work. God said He will help if we trust in His plan, "Submit yourselves therefore, to God. Resist the devil, and he will flee from you", *James 4:7 KJV*.

"I have decided to stick with love. Hate is too great a burden to bear" *Martin Luther King, Jr.* Hate for another was never a part of the plan, God would never burden you with such a thing; all he does is for your good; there is no good in hating another; it's the absence of love for another; it's being without God since God is love. "Those who hate the truth will buy into this type of deception, precipitating their ultimate destruction. Meanwhile, believers must stand firm, holding tightly to the truth. In a world of falsehood and deliberate deception, we must always be on guard", *Crosswalk.com*. We tend to focus on our particular circumstances rather than the promises of God. For several years, God has been true to His Word. We sometimes get discouraged during the challenging times in life; we must remember the rainbow, the sign God showed Noah that symbolizes a promise. (*Genesis 9:12-17*) Trust in His Plan.

satan, in his subtle ways, has strategically placed his soldiers to combat and take down the belief in God. For e*xample:* The USA is (*in words only*), a country built on "In God We Trust" (*perception is not always reality*), but yet, God is the only one this country does not trust, until tragedy strikes. satan has moved foreigners to this country; people against Jesus being the Son of God, and are against God; now that they are citizens of this country, they now have a right to freedom of religion as the Constitution states. See, this is what subtle is; (*especially* *of a change or distinction so delicate or precise, as to be difficult to analyze or describe)*. Now, satan and his soldiers have changed things. Now you can't pray, using the name of Jesus in public; you can't say God (*without challenge, but, you can say the universe in place of God*) in public; you can't display a sign at school or in a public building that acknowledge God or Jesus, and all this, in a country, that lead you to believe it's foundation was built on "In God We Trust" (*perception is not always reality*). None of this is intended as hate speech against foreigners, but to show how deception works subtly. God has a plan, even for this; trust in His plan. "The devil has no power ... except in the dark." *Cassandra Clare.*

Psalms 119 tells how God can speak spiritual light into our hearts, to help us. Exposure to His voice – in His Word – will help us discern the difference between the good light of God and that which is not. When people do not trust in His plan, they wander in darkness and often become angry at God, refusing to come to Him for help. This is how satan's masquerade as an angel of light is so effective; It gets some believing that God is the liar, and that God is the source of darkness; Then, in their distress, they focus their hatred towards the only one who can save them.

"Darkness and light are metaphors for evil and good. An angel of light will automatically seem to be a good being, for the parallelism of evil with darkness, and of good with light, is a pattern of thought in human history," u*nknown*. In the Bible, light is a spiritual metaphor for truth and God's unchanging nature. "For God, who commanded the light to shine out of darkness, hath shined in our hearts, to give the light of the knowledge of the glory of God in the face of Jesus Christ", *2 Corinthians 4:6 KJV.* When we read *"satan disguises himself as an angel of light,"* This is another of his subtle attempts to get you focused on your love of the light; this is deception.

satan wants you to think that he is good, truthful, loving, and powerful; all the things that God is (*2 Thessalonians 2*). To portray himself as a dark, devilish being with horns would not be very appealing to the majority. Most people are not drawn to darkness but to light. Therefore, satan appears as a creature of light to draw us to himself and his lies. "And no marvel; for satan himself is transformed into an angel of light", *2 Corinthians 11:14 KJV*. The knowledge of Christ must transform our lives so that our attitudes and actions will "honor God". This is His plan. God has redeemed us; we are to fix our faith on the coming of "the *blessed hope of the coming of Christ*", not the angel of light.

"The devil keeps man from good a thousand ways; so that when he seeks to do good, he pierces him with his shafts; when he desires to embrace God with his whole heart in love, he subjects him to several tribulations, seeking to pervert his mind and his good work before God. And when he seeks virtue, the devil tells him that he does not know what he is doing, and he teaches him that he can set his own law for himself", *Hildegard Of Bingen*. *Isaiah 8* paints a picture of the darkness that results from ignoring God's word. Walking in darkness is attempting to find truth without the word of God. Don't look to mediums and wizards, consulting the dead on behalf of the living. "We are all acquainted with demons, aren't we? Sometimes they are more subtle than the devil in person. They are things that clutch at us, strangle us, and force us to obey them. They control us with great delight, and finally, they own us. Demons are certainly as much around today as they were in Jesus' day. They are more subtle, perhaps, and so we think we have outgrown them. Because we call them by other names, we miss them. But there is still a great force surrounding us that tries to push us into what is not of God", *Macrina Wiederkehr, Ephesians 6:12*

"But we speak the wisdom of God in a mystery, even the hidden wisdom, which God ordained before the world unto our glory: Which none of the princes of this world knew: for had they known it, they would not have crucified the Lord of glory. But as it is written, Eye hath not seen, nor ear heard, neither have entered into the heart of man, the things which God hath prepared for them that love him", *1 Corinthians 2:7-9 KJV*. Trust in His Plan.

satan, the god of this world, has tempted mankind to follow his pride instead of the ways of Christ. In *Matthew 4*, he tempted the character of Jesus; all the suggestions he made would have been selfish acts if Jesus had yielded, and would have caused Him to act as man would (*abuse power*) if man had that type of power. satan sets the agenda; the unbelieving world follows, and mankind continues to be deceived. He attempted to get Jesus to forsake His mission to save the lost souls; satan wanted Jesus to execute His divine power to escape suffering and death on the cross; this would have allowed satan to win more souls over to his team. satan deceives us into thinking our free will is our independence from the laws of God; he wants us to believe we have the right to judge what is right or wrong for us. God's law is based on His righteousness, but by His grace, we are made righteous.

God's plan is for us to focus on the future rather than the past, although the past is also important because it shows how God has always delivered on His promises. We are to keep our hopes on what He has promised for the future. God veiled Himself in a human body (*Jesus*) so that we might know Him in a personal way; He lived among us to feel what we feel, see as we see, and experience as we experience. Jesus made the point "the Father and I are one" so that we might know that He is God in the flesh. Jesus said that He is coming back to end this; to collect the believers: those who held fast and didn't quit believing; not giving in to the deception of the devil. As stated before, satan will not appear to you as he is portrayed in paintings with horns and a pitchfork; he is the angel of light; he wants you to believe he is good (*deception*). "The greatest trick the devil ever pulled was convincing the world that he doesn't exist", *Charles Baudelaire*.

satan: the god of this world *2 Corinthians 4:4;* no, he's not in hell yet; making it appear (*deception*) as if the constitution is Bible-based, but let us look closely at the outcome of the constitution; *the end pre-exists in the means.* This is the gateway for him to get his believers in place and power for his world system to work. With this plan, nonbelievers from other nations (*nonbelievers, idol worshipers, enemies of God*) can become citizens of this country with the right to deny you from worshiping God because they claim to be offended. Go to where they are from and try that; see what happens. Think about it! Again, this is not hate towards them, but the subtlety of deception.

The deception of satan has many fooled into thinking that they can live without laws, that they are naturally moral, and that God has dictated that you keep statutes that He knows you can't keep. Can you imagine satan telling Eve (*for illustration only*): "If God didn't want you to eat from that tree, why did he put it there to tease you? He's just a trickster; go ahead and do your thing, girl; eat that fruit". But we forget that laws are to show us how immoral we are without grace. All God warned us not to do are things that do us no good, and if we believe that God seeks our greatest good, then we shouldn't be deceived into thinking that He doesn't want us to enjoy life; with all these laws, rules, and so forth. Deception has many believing that we would be better off without policemen (*until they need one*); believing; they are all corrupt (*so are some politicians, but somehow, they just keep getting voted into office*) and are just keeping us from doing what we want to do; they keep us from speeding, stealing, burglarizing, robbery, driving drunk, beating up wives, and so forth. They put you in jail for these things; I dare them; this is my life, and I should be able to live it as messed up as I want to. Some say: do away with the laws, and the enforcers thereof, we will all carry guns and shoot each other when we feel it is right. Be careful what you ask for because that is exactly what is happening today.

When you come to know (*and I pray that you do*) that God's law acts as a mirror, it allows you to see the vanity in what you are doing, and how grace comes into play. The laws He gave to Moses in *Exodus 20 KJV* are as follows: *1)* "Thou shalt have no other gods before me". Worshipping created things has no value; it keeps your focus on self, physical pleasure, work, money, etc, temporal things, but does not seek your greatest good. 2) "Thou shalt not make unto thee any graven image". They do nothing for you; only you do for them, and your love for them cannot be reciprocated because they are not alive. However, the Ark of the Covenant was not to be an object of worship either. When the Israelites carried it into war like a cult idol, assuming it would guarantee victory, they were defeated, suffering 30,000 casualties. The Ark was captured and taken to the temple of a foreign god. 3) "Thou shalt not take the name of the Lord thy god in vain" Simply put, God is saying; don't abuse my name; you can use it, but don't abuse it, you know, when you say things like: "I swear by the name of God, that I will cut you if you take another step". Using the name is only effective if you know Him and He knows you. For *example*, you can call (*fictional*) Candy Man or Bloody Mary so many times, and they appear, but with them comes sorrow. If you know God and He knows you, when you call Him, He will come, but no sorrow follows Him, only blessings, except when you call His name in vain. Do not empty God's name of its holiness, authenticity, or truth. 4) "Remember the Sabbath day, to keep it holy". "The Sabbath was made for man, not man for the Sabbath."(*Mark 2:27 KJV*).With compassion, Christ declares the Sabbath for doing good rather than harm; for saving life rather than killing (*Mark 3:4*). The Sabbath is to be kept holy unto the Lord (*reverent honor and homage paid to God*); with prepared hearts (*adoring reverence or regard*); rest from concentrating on your thoughts about your worldly employments and recreations. Spend time in the public and private exercises of His worship (*Formal or ceremonious rendering of such honor and homage*), and in the duties of necessity and mercy (*Isaiah 58:13 KJV*). For those who choose to observe the Sabbath, neither should you; make unnecessary demands on others that would hinder them from observing the Lord's Day. But at the same time, don't be like those whom Jesus spoke to in *Matthew 12:1-14 KJV*; they misunderstood the Mosaic Law; they made the observance of the Sabbath more rigorous than God had commanded. 5) "Honour thy father and thy mother" (*regard with great respect; have high respect; es-*

teem). The commandment itself encourages obedience. "Since, therefore, the name of Father is a sacred one, and is transferred to men by the peculiar goodness of God; the dishonoring of parents redounds to the dishonor of God Himself", *John Calvin*. It is not to be interpreted to mean that only if your father and mother are good parents. "However unworthy of honor a father may be, he still retains, since he is a father, his right over his children, provided it does not in anywise derogate from the judgment of God; for it is too absurd to think of absolving under any pretext the sins which are condemned by His Law; nay, it would be a base profanation to misuse the name of father for the covering of sins", *John Calvin*. In other words, honor them, but not to the point of breaking God's law; do not allow your love for them to become more important than love for God. Now, when it comes to the matter of obeying your parents, if they ask you to stop believing that God is and start worshiping idols, then this commandment only requires that you honor them as your father and mother in this regard, but not to obey that request; that request causes you to break God's law. 6) "Thou shalt not kill". Do not participate in a destructive activity or kill anyone outside the context of war with a weapon. The shedding of innocent blood is a direct offense against God since man is made in God's image. A person who breaks into your home and threatens you and your family, or any person who threatens to cause you great harm; these are not innocent; you act in self-defense. But, to kill another with a weapon just because you feel like it is just evil. 7)" Thou shalt not commit adultery". Sexual misconduct: plain and simple. Treat marriage as a relationship that excludes sexual intimacy (*physical or mental*) with other persons. Fidelity to husband or wife during marriage, what else can we say? 8) "Thou shalt not steal". Unauthorized taking of private property. To acquire something honestly and lawfully is what we should desire. If you endeavor to grow rich by injustice, you have stolen; if you plunder your neighbor of their goods, that your own may be increased from what you have dishonestly taken, you have stolen. "Desire leads to coveting; coveting leads to stealing," *Maimonides*. 9) "Thou shalt not bear false witness against thy neighbour" Speaking falsely in any matter, lying; using ambiguous or unclear expressions, usually to avoid commitment. "By malignant or vicious detraction, we sin against our neighbor's good name: by lying, sometimes even by casting a slur upon him, we injure him in his estate." *John Calvin. 10)*" Thou shalt not covet". Do not have wrongful desire or craving for something that belongs to someone else, or scheming to take it. Love should regulate our wishes and desires. "We must know that God does not wish that you deprive your neighbor of anything that belongs to them so that they suffer the loss and you gratify your avarice (*An excessive or inordinate desire of gain*) with it", *Martin Luther*.

Faith is: believing God and acting like you believe God. The works of God in the world are accomplished by faith. The heroes of faith, in *Hebrews 11*, show that when God spoke, they acted accordingly. You have to believe to trust, which leads to having faith. You must believe to obey, as you have seen in the past; if people don't believe, they won't obey, and trust in His plan.

The next time you go to a funeral, you are tempted to ask the question; why did God take them so soon, or why did God take them away from me? *This indicates that you are familiar with God's sovereignty, and your grief is responsible for this question.* If you ask the question, where is God now? (*Indicating anger towards Him*). Am I being punished? (*Chances are, you don't know Him as the sovereign God*). Depending on where you are, your knowledge of who God is will determine your response to a loss (*outside of your normal grief*). When you learn to trust in His plan, you will begin to understand that certain things are necessary for the greater cause (*His plan*). Remember, God is seeking your greatest good. Whatever hurts wasn't necessarily designed to hurt you, but because you loved that individual, you experience hurt. God will comfort those who have faith in Him, *helping through His word, leading them to see His plan,* helping them achieve spiritual prosperity in their time of loss; that comes from a right relationship with

God. This spiritual relationship helps you understand that all physical things come to a finish. The matter of sin is spiritual; without the shedding of blood, there is no forgiveness of sin (*Hebrews 9:22 KJV*). "All have sinned and fallen short of the glory of God" (*Romans 3:23 KJV*), and "the wages of sin is death" (*Romans 6:23 KJV*). Wherever there is sin, someone must die spiritually. The death that Christ suffered was placed on our account. His death can count for ours, and we do not have to die spiritually. Faith is how this transaction takes place. Whoever believes in Jesus will not perish but will have eternal life. (*John 3:16KJV*). Aren't you glad He has a plan? Trust in His plan.

satan, in all his deceptive ways, will convince some that injustice needs to be met with violence. *Romans 12:19 KJV* "Dearly beloved, avenge not yourselves, but rather give place unto wrath (*but leave room for God's wrath*): for it is written, Vengeance is mine; I will repay, saith the Lord". Vengeance in this sense is righteous judgment. *Deuteronomy 32:35* To me belongeth vengeance, and recompense; their foot shall slide in due time: for the day of their calamity is at hand, and the things that shall come upon them make haste. The purpose of Christ's death was to be a sacrifice that united all in one salvation (*Ephesians 2:11-22 KJV*), to bring us to the point of being on one accord. The opposition between races and all nations should cease. God is calling us to "become all things to all men that by all means we might save some" (*1 Corinthians 9:22 KJV*). We are to make disciples of all nations (*Matthew 28:19 KJV*). We cannot do that if we don't love all nations, all peoples, and all cultures. That is a challenge we can only succeed in with help from the loving Spirit of God, who has poured out God's love in our hearts (*Romans 5:5 KJV*). Trust in His Plan. *Genesis 37* tells how Jacob's preferential treatment of Joseph in no way condones the brothers actions; it points out to us that we should love all men as Christ would. When individuals feel that love, it makes it easier for them to love others in return. Joseph trusted in God's plan. *1 Kings 19* tells the story of Elijah fleeing from Jezebel after a victory over the prophets of Baal. Elijah fears for his own life; God does not cause him to feel belittled, but rather, He ministers to him quietly, restoring his spirit and strength. Then Elijah began to regain his trust in God's plan. God cares when we are hurt and discouraged; He gently calls us to Himself and restores us.

Most likely, it was David's reputation that prompted Solomon to write in Proverbs *22:1 KJV*: "A good name is to be chosen rather than great riches." Each of us must take this Scripture to heart and dedicate ourselves to developing a blameless reputation, by being fair, just, and righteous; by being true to our word. *1 Kings 5* David and Solomon trusted in God's Plan. Spiritual battles explode before our very eyes, but we neither see them nor hear them, we have no clue as to what goes on in the spiritual realm (*Daniel 10:13*). Guardian angels minister: to our needs (*Hebrews 1:14*). We entertain angels "unaware" (*Hebrews 13:2*). The spiritual realm is real; without the Scriptures, we would know little about it. The Syrian army is camped around Dothan, but Elisha (*2 Kings 6 KJV*) is not concerned because an army of the angels of the Lord encircles the horizon. Walking by faith, not by sight, is trusting in His plan. Israel experienced many miracles on their route to the promised land. God delivered on His promise on every occasion, giving them victories and driving the inhabitants from the land, and God used insects to secure their victory so that they did not have to fight. But, somewhere in all that, they forgot what God was able to do. When they discovered the giants on the land, they started trippin' *Numbers 13*. When we are obedient to God, nothing can touch us that doesn't come from God Himself; this is why satan had to get permission in *Job 1*. God is jealous to care for His beloved people; God offers **the obedient** full protection in spiritual warfare. Of course, obedience is putting on His full armor and standing firm, knowing that we will triumph in Him only, trusting in His plan.

satan will deceive you into thinking that it is okay to kick against the prick, but when you do, it only hurts you. An "Oxgoad" *is a long (typically 8–10 feet) wooden staff tipped with a sharp metal spike, historically used by farmers to prod, guide, and drive oxen during plowing. The farmer would prick the animal to steer it in the right direction. Sometimes the animal would rebel by kicking out at the prick, and this would result in the prick being driven even further into its flesh. In essence, the more an ox rebelled, the more it suffered.* God ordered your steps to steer you in the right direction; the more you kick against his order, you're driving the prick in deeper and deeper, now becoming a losing battle. satan's plan is: to keep you far from the truth; without direction; believing that you don't have to follow God's plan; it only leads to you having no will of your own; it is Deception. Some battles we take on are worthless; getting the victory does nothing for us; for a moment, it feels good, but that's it. Now, you ask yourself: why did I do that? It gained me nothing. "It's like taking candy from a baby." Only the blood of Christ can pay for our sins. And only confession can restore fellowship with God. Trust in His plan. "Vision is not enough; it must be combined with venture. It is not enough to stare up the steps; we must step up the stairs", *Vaclav Havel.*

Chapter 14

Integrity
(*Are you who you thought you were?*)

    Integrity is defined as adherence to moral and ethical principles; it could be explained as remaining fixed and conforming to a standard of right behavior, sanctioned by acceptable fundamental essence, producing a given quality, the quality of being complete, wholesome, and unimpaired. If this is the case, many don't know the meaning of integrity, as they thought they did. When a person does not adhere to moral or ethical principles, does not stay conformed to standard right behavior, lacks soundness and moral character, and is not honest, and accuses someone of insulting their integrity, they do not know the meaning of integrity. We all should be people of integrity and honor. The Bible defines it as the girdle of truth (*integrity holds things in place*). Based on the type of clothing worn during the time this was written, before any vigorous activity, the loose ends of clothing (*tunics, cloaks, mantles, etc.*) had to be gathered up and tucked into the wide band worn around the midsection of the body. The band (*usually about six inches wide*) also served as a kind of pocket or pouch to carry personal items such as a dagger, money, or other things. "Gird up your mind" or "*gird up your heart*" are variants of this phrase and call for mental or spiritual preparation for a coming challenge. "Stand therefore, having your loins girt about with truth, and having on the breastplate of righteousness", *Ephesians 6:14 KJV*; Truth is not just knowledge about facts. Truth is integrity in the inner person. Once you decide to believe in a moral and ethical principle, you should stick to it. Be steadfast and unmovable, always remembering wholesomeness, completeness, and unimpaired by other influences (*influences against these principles*).

"The more man meditates upon good thoughts, the better will be his world and the world at large", *Confucius*. To treat another as though they were less than human is not moral or ethical. To treat another differently, as to how you would want to be treated, is not wholesomeness or completeness. To do part good, and part bad, is not wholesome either. Let me explain: a driver strictly adheres to the posted speed limit until the light turns red, as the driver approaches the light, they speed up and run the light. That's not integrity. If you love and treat others as you would have them do unto you, then you are on the verge of understanding integrity. Is it okay to do wrong if no one knows you did wrong? If you have integrity, the answer should be no. Imagine: going through an active school zone; no policeman in sight; just you; no other cars around; you zip right on through without slowing to the school zone speed limit; ignoring the flashing lights. If you believe that's okay, then where is your integrity? "No matter how fast light travels, it finds the darkness has always got there first, and is waiting for it", *Terry Pratchett*. According to *Genesis 1*, darkness never left, but was separated from light. Light expels darkness; it has no power when the light is on. Integrity is like keeping the light on. If we always do right, even when we are alone, we are practicing before we face the judgment of others. "The Christian virtue of self-control is the consistent ability to say "no" to our appetites and to live in moderation. It is motivated by a desire for single-minded worship of God and holiness ("for it helps guard against greed and idolatry; a holiness which itself springs from a love for God and is accompanied by joy, not a hatred for all desire and passion"), *Crosswalk.com.*

"The soul that is within me no man can degrade", *Frederick Douglass.* At times, we don't realize how much control we have over others. For example; If you stop at a traffic light; there is a street just before the light; you get there first and stop just short of blocking the intersection, (*some have a sign asking you not to block the intersection*) well, because you stopped, then the cars after you, will most likely stop also (*of course, there is always one that is not paying attention, and when the smoke clears, that will be the only one that did not stop and will be standing all alone feeling foolish*), leaving the intersection open for people to enter and cross or to turn in front of you while waiting for the light to change. You can't go until the light changes anyway, right? If you, the first, don't stop, the rest will not stop. You have control; you made others aware of what was right without telling them they did wrong; you led them into righteousness.

A test is not only for the instructor but also for the learner. A math test helps one know what they understand about math, a science test helps one know what they understand about science, and so forth; it also helps the instructor know if their instructional methods are sufficient for learning. When God allows us to be tested, it is not for Him to discover where we are, but for us to know if we are who we thought we were. Are we a people of integrity, or is it only what we wear on the outside, for others to see? Remember, perception is not always reality. "The ultimate measure of a man is not where he stands in moments of comfort and convenience, but where he stands at times of challenge and controversy", *Martin Luther King Jr.*

The absence of integrity is hard to hide when a person speaks. "If you wish to know the mind of a man, listen to his words", *Chinese proverb.* What are your habits? What do you do behind closed doors? Just as you have curtains in your home to keep the light out, is your life the same? Paul says, "For we were formerly darkness, but now, we are the light in the Lord". Do not be afraid of the light; it will allow you to walk in love just as Jesus did. "Even though you are on the right track, you will get run over if you just sit there", *Will Rogers.* Growing into integrity is not easy; a lot of self has to be released for you to grow. "Without a struggle, there can be no progress. Those who profess to favor freedom, and disapprove agitation, are like people who want crops without plowing up the ground, they want rain without thunder and lightning", *Frederick Douglass.* We can still demand justice and agitate the powers that be, with integrity; the storms of life are what make us strong and strengthen our integrity (*that's if you had integrity before the storm began*). Don't let your good be [become the cause of slander, gossip, or offense]evil spoken of (*Romans 14:16*).

"Human progress is neither automatic nor inevitable. Every step toward the goal of justice requires sacrifice, suffering, and struggle; the tireless exertions and passionate concern of dedicated individuals", *Martin Luther King, Jr.* This type of dedication requires a person of integrity. To involve yourself in a struggle for any form of justice, you MUST first have INTEGRITY and MORAL COURAGE as Daniel did. *Daniel 1.* Jesus is our shepherd, who leads us into righteousness because our abilities and intelligence cannot meet the demands of life. Without Jesus leading (*The example of His life*), we cannot be a people of integrity. When we grow to love others unconditionally, as we would have them love us, then, the verge of understanding integrity is at hand; this is what we should pray for daily. "People who say it cannot be done should not interrupt those who are doing it", *Chinese Proverb.*

There would be more integrity in marriages if the wedding vows read: do you promise to seek the other's greatest good; will you always consider the other's welfare; will you always try to understand the other's point of view; will you be committed to the relationship no matter what? Will you promise to keep everybody else out of the business that should only concern this husband and wife? True love dictates that any problem, situation, or bump in the road of life should be worked out between the two of you with God as the Judge. People who spend the majority of their marriage in therapy or counseling don't need to be married; *the end preexists in the means.* If you have to pay someone to mediate the relationship continually, then where is the integrity of the marriage? This means one or both don't want to be truly committed behind the wall of submission. Long story short, God did not join you together; you did. Remember, integrity is defined as adherence to moral and ethical principles and could be explained as: remaining fixed and conforming to a standard of right behavior, sanctioned by acceptable fundamental essence, producing a given quality, the quality of being complete, wholesome, and unimpaired by influences opposite to these values. "If you don't have integrity, you have nothing. You can't buy it. You can have all the money in the world, but if you are not a moral and ethical person, you really have nothing", *Henry Kravis.* Awareness is the key to the truth, and the truth will set you free. "Well done is better than well said", *Benjamin Franklin*

Chapter 15

Giving
(Have I helped someone in need today?)

Give because you have a yearning to do so; you desire to help make someone whole again, seeking their greatest good. God created the heavens and the earth (*Genesis 1*) before He formed man. God gave His best, knowing that we would not reciprocate the love He put into the creation. After each phase of creation, God looked at His work and said, "It is good" (*Genesis 1:10, 12, and 18 KJV*), which is Him assuring that what He gave was His best. God gave the best of what He knew man would need before man knew he needed it, seeking his greatest good. This is how to give out of love. Giving is not always financial, but most often the two are put together. Who would venture to say that giving has nothing to do with money? It has only to do with Agape love; Agape love causes you to give of yourself without reciprocation; you gave because you wanted to; you have grown in the love of giving. When we value spiritual things, we freely support spiritual things. We give of ourselves and our finances; we give up private time to study God's word, attending Bible class, etc. When we value temporal things, we resent giving to spiritual things; we are not willing to give of ourselves or our finances to spiritual things; we are not willing to give up our private time for the learning of what God expects of us.

But, will give to worldly things; all your time and money. Not willing to help local ministries by donating time or money to outreach ministries, but are willing to spend money on rims that are worth more than your vehicle and buy clothes that don't fit; you know, males with clothes too big; females with clothes too small. Too often, we place our faith in money, not in God, who supplies money through various sources that He made available. I know you're thinking, I work for the money I earn. God didn't give me that; as stated before, God provides those resources that you use to earn money. "But remember the Lord your God, for it is he who gives you the ability to produce wealth, and so confirms his covenant, which he swore to your ancestors, as it is today", *Deuteronomy 8:18 NIV*. We, at times, allow what we know to be overshadowed by what we don't know. We make important decisions based on what we don't know. "O Lord, I know the way of man is not in himself; it is not in man who walks to direct his own steps. O Lord, correct me, but with justice; Not in Your anger, lest you bring me to nothing" *(Jeremiah 10:23-24 KJV)*. If you don't know that God expects you to be a giver, then your decision not to give is based on what you don't know. If you know that God expects this and don't give, then you are robbing God and cheating yourself. *(Matthew 6:2-3 KJV)* tells that God expects us to give. The first part of verse 2, "Therefore when" indicates an expectancy. "² Therefore when thou doest thine alms, do not sound a trumpet before thee, as the hypocrites do in the synagogues and, in the streets, that they may have glory of men. Verily I say unto you, they have their reward. ³ But when thou doest alms, let not thy left hand know what thy right hand doeth:"

God has shown that He can be completely trusted with all your needs. "Trust in the Lord, and do good; dwell in the land, and feed on His faithfulness. Delight yourself also in the Lord. He shall give you the desires of your heart. Commit your way to the Lord. Trust also in Him, and He shall bring it to pass. He shall bring forth your righteousness as the light and your justice as the noonday" *(Psalm 37:3-6 KJV)*. The desires of a clean heart He created in you is how I see it.

If you don't believe, you won't obey; obedience is built on the foundation of belief. If you truly believe God is, and He is good all the time, all He does is for our benefit, you should obey whatever He asks of you, because when you doubt, obedience is hard for you. You cannot share the word of God if you don't truly believe His word. It is hard to convince unbelievers if faith is missing from your life. You must know that you know who God is, and walk and speak in that.

Deuteronomy 26 shows the importance of giving. In gratitude for what He has given us, we should offer a portion back to God. If we know who He is, the Creator, we will understand that everything is His anyway. His goodness, compassion, and love are by His choosing, not obligation; God answers to no other; He is because He is; He provides us with the things we need, and sometimes what we want. *2 Corinthians 8:9-15 TLB* shows what giving relates to love. "You know how full of love and kindness our Lord Jesus was: though he was so very rich, yet to help you he became so very poor, so that by being poor he could make you rich. I want to suggest that you finish what you started a year ago, for you were not only the first to propose this idea, but the first to begin doing something about it. Having started the ball rolling so enthusiastically, you should carry this project through to completion just as gladly, giving whatever you can out of whatever you have. Let your enthusiastic idea at the start be equalled by your realistic action now. If you are really eager to give, then it isn't important how much you have to give. God wants you to give what you have, not what you haven't. Of course, I don't mean that those who receive your gifts should have an easy time of it at your expense, but you should divide with them. Right now, you have plenty and can help them; then, at some other time, they can share with you when you need it. In this way, each will have as much as he needs. Do you remember what the Scriptures say about this? "He that gathered much had nothing left over, and he that gathered little had enough." So you also should share with those in need".

You cannot love without giving of yourself. Some have a desire to be known as the gift-giver, for recognition rather than as a giver who desires to help. Some people will not give unless they get recognized for their gift; they donated money to the church and the pastor didn't mention their name (*the devil just arrived*); "Honey, I won't be giving anything else to this church; pastor didn't mention my donation; the deacons must have kept it for themselves or the pastor kept it". satan will always be there looking for an opportunity to cause conflict. "Be helpful even if there's no immediate profit in it", *Susan Ward*.

If your giving is out of love, then mentioning your gift is of no value to you because that was not the foundation for your giving. You gave because it was needed, and you were able to meet a need. Praise God for that! *Psalm 50:10-11, 14-15 KJV* states: "For every beast of the forest is Mine, and the cattle on a thousand hills. I know all the birds of the mountains, and the wild beasts of the field are mine. . . Offer to God thanksgiving, and pay your vows to Him. "Call upon Me in the day of trouble; I will deliver you, and you shall glorify Me".

"The most important thing in life is to learn how to give out love and to let it come in", *Morrie Schwartz*. Giving is not always about physical things; giving unselfishly is dedication to the welfare of those in need of words of wisdom, encouragement, enlightenment, etc., common welfare, and seeking their greatest good. *Deuteronomy 15:7-11 KJV* says: "But you shall open your hand to him and lend him sufficient for his need, whatever it may be", sometimes that might be words of wisdom; teaching them a trade, etc., but not always money. To give a poor man money is a waste if you fail to teach him how to increase what you gave him, so that he may graduate to a better state of living. You did not help him; all you did was give him money; when it's gone, he will still be poor. Teach methods of rehabilitation before giving money, so they understand what you are giving and why; they need to understand that your objective is to get them back on their feet, not to see you only as the one who gives them money; you will forever be a crutch to them. Seek to know how they got to this state;

pray for guidance, ask God how; you should help them, maybe pay a bill or buy them food or gas, etc., Wait for an answer from God before you place money in their hands because; God might reveal to you that what they are asking you for is not what they need at all; they just might be looking for a crutch."Behold, I send you forth as sheep in the midst of wolves: be ye therefore wise as serpents, and harmless as doves" *Matthew 10:16 KJV*.

"What we do for ourselves dies with us. What we do for others and the world remains and is immortal", *Albert Pike.*

The question has been asked: "If God is all that, why does He need money?" God does not need money; all is His. If it's money given to the church that is in question, then I will try to explain. Since I am not a theologian or a scholar, consider this with an open mind. **One view** is: "tithing of the produce of the land collected every third year for the local Levites (*the Levites who had no inheritance in Canaan*), orphans, strangers, and widows". **Another view** is: *Malachi 3:10 KJV*, "that there be meat in mine house", which was to help feed, clothe, and shelter the man of God in his efforts to bring meat (*the word of God*). It was done out of love, one for another, to help him distribute the word of God. In ancient times, special storehouses were established in the temple to receive the tithes of the harvest. If the people were not faithful, the priests could not serve and perform their duties. Free will offerings were for the buildings, and to help the church help others; having resources to aid one another as the need arises, that the church may have it to distribute". I know; some only; build bigger buildings and can't afford to help people because; they are in debt. "Tithe contributions were to represent the life of the giver, which ensured the availability of meat (*spiritual Food*) in God's storehouse to nurture the life of the giver. The "meat" in God's "storehouse" must be distributed. **Another view** states that Israel was obligated to support their national workers (*priests*), their holidays (*festivals*), and their poor (*strangers, widows, and orphans*) through their annual tithes. **Yet, another view:** In *Matthew 23:23 KJV*, "Jesus criticized the Pharisees for treating tithing as more important than mercy, love, justice, and faithfulness, but not for tithing itself. These were customs and rituals from the Old Testament that were nailed to the cross with Jesus so that they could no longer condemn us." Okay, enough of that. I'm sure you see now how this thinking can wrap you up, causing you to lose sight of what is important, and end up like the Pharisees to whom Jesus was speaking. The new covenant gives us justification and peace with God. How much more should we be willing to give freely and generously to the church so God's work can be done in the world? This is the function of God's stewards, not a commandment. "Charity looks at the need and not at the cause", *German Proverb*. But, the giving to those in need, the less fortunate, the poor, etc is a commandment as stated in *John 13:*" I am giving you a new commandment, that you love one another. Just as I have loved you, so you too are to love one another", *John 13:34 AMP*. This also allows us to reciprocate God's love for us. "A person whose mind is quiet and satisfied in God is in the pathway to health", *Ellen G. White*.

16 Chapter

Forgiveness
(How soon we forget)

Forgiveness is the intentional and voluntary process by which a victim changes feelings and attitudes regarding an offense and lets go of negative emotions such as vengefulness, with an increased ability to wish the offender well.

Matthew 6:11-15 states: For if ye forgive men their trespasses, your heavenly Father will also forgive you: But if ye forgive not men their trespasses, neither will your Father forgive your trespasses. *Matthew 18* states: Jesus saith unto him, I say not unto thee, until seven times: (*forgiving thy brother*) but seventy times seven. The parable was told about the king who forgave a debt of a servant, but the same servant went out, and found one of his fellow servants, who owed him: and he laid hands on him, and took him by the throat, saying: Pay me that thou owest (*how soon we forget!*). And his fellow servant fell at his feet, and besought him, saying: Have patience with me, and I will pay thee all. And he would not, but went and cast him into prison, till he should pay the debt. Then his lord, after that, he had called him, said unto him, O thou wicked servant, I forgave thee all that debt, because thou desiredst me: shouldest not thou also have had compassion on thy fellow servant, even as I pitied thee? And his lord was wroth and delivered him to the tormentors, till he should pay all that was due unto him. So likewise shall my heavenly Father do also unto you, if ye from your hearts forgive not every one of his brother their trespasses. Forgiveness in view of grace should promote repentance on the offender's part. *Repentance: deep sorrow, compunction, or contrition for a past sin, wrongdoing, or the like; Also regret for any past actions.* The Bible uses this definition, but also defines it as changing one's way of thinking. "Mistakes are always forgivable, if one has the courage to admit them", *Bruce Lee.*

"Take heed to yourselves: If thy brother trespass against thee, rebuke him; *and if he repent,* forgive him. And if he trespass against thee seven times in a day, and seven times in a day turn again to thee, saying, *I repent*; thou shalt forgive him" *Luke 17:3-4 KJV.* It's impossible to be transformed if we don't admit our sin; pride controls one without repentance, and pride leads to destruction. If we set pride aside, then repentance becomes the responsibility of the offender, and pardon becomes the responsibility of the offended, which makes it a two-way process. Keep in mind that if the offender doesn't repent, you still have to love them even with the issue unsettled, but not hang out like buddies. The wrong that was committed is their burden, not yours. Do not allow them to cause you to feel guilty for something they did to you when all they have to do is admit they wronged you; God's grace produces repentance in us. "So repent [change your inner self—your old way of thinking, regret past sins] and return [to God—seek His purpose for your life], so that your sins may be wiped away [blotted out, completely erased], so that times of refreshing may come from the presence of the Lord [restoring you like a cool wind on a hot day]", *Acts 3:19 AMP.*

"Darkness cannot drive out darkness; only light can do that. Hate cannot drive out hate; only love can do that", *Martin Luther King, Jr.* It takes great power to forgive, and this power comes only from God. Forgiveness is the key to replacing anger and hatred with love. How can a person truly love without the power to forgive? If you have never loved, then you can't judge someone who loves. If you have never forgiven someone, it would be unfair for you to judge someone who forgives. All who love the same thing don't love it the same way; their method of affection will differ, and all who hate the same thing don't hate it the same way; their method of hate will differ. When God forgives us, that level of forgiveness, only we and God know the total worth. No one person can say he or she has been forgiven for something far worse than what you have ever done; it is hard for their mind to grasp that the bubble gum you stole is the same as the ten million dollars they stole. In God's eyes, they both stole and stealing is stealing, and God said "thou shalt not steal". "Nothing so strong as gentleness, nothing so gentle as real strength," *St Francis de Sales.*

Galatians 6 KJV states; Brethren, if a man be overtaken in a fault, ye which are spiritual, restore such an one in the spirit of meekness; considering thyself, lest thou also be tempted (*how soon we forget!*). It takes a lot of power to practice meekness or gentleness; these, too, come from God; the two are often categorized as weaknesses, which is far from the truth. Meek and gentle, "power under control," and this, too, comes only from God. Since God is willing to forgive us, we should be willing to practice forgiveness until we become better at it, practice, practice, practice. Instead of passing judgment, try practicing forgiveness. Practicing forgiveness does not leave much room for a superiority attitude. When one believes they are superior to another, forgiveness is canceled out. Forgiveness comes easily when we learn to love. If we believe heaven is our destination, then we can't get there without the ability to love or forgive. To serve God requires selflessness (*Daniel 3; when the three were placed in the furnace, because they would not bow down to an idol god*). Selflessness is what we must achieve to forgive. It is hard to forgive another when all you remember is what they did to you (*selfishness*). In fact, if you spend time thinking about the whole picture. What did I contribute to this cause? Could I be the reason they did what they did to me? If I had not been doing what I was doing, I might not have been where I was, and what happened might not have happened. After all this, the focus has shifted to the whole rather than just what happened to you. This is not to say it is your fault, but to say you evaluated the situation carefully before deciding to forgive (grace) or not, and whether the offender is experiencing true repentance, or yanking your chain. "We cannot embrace God's forgiveness if we are so busy clinging to past wounds and nursing old grudges", *T. D. Jakes.* Awareness is the key to the truth, and the truth will set your mind free.

"You meant evil against me, but God meant it for good" *Genesis 50:20 KJV.*

Genesis 45 tells us how Joseph reminds us of where we would be without forgiveness; without forgiving and being forgiven. Joseph was willing to forgive the very ones who, some years earlier, had plotted to kill him. Joseph's ability to forgive (show grace) was rooted in his theology: If we seek the eternal rather than temporal, we can more easily forgive when someone robs us of temporal things. When God takes over a life, He makes a difference; the worse the life, the greater the change. Being forgiven has different outcomes for each of us. The level of a thing that we have done against another is always different. Where would we be without grace, mercy, and forgiveness? Because of human weakness, sustaining a relationship without messing up is hard for us. We all eventually need to forgive and to be forgiven because vanity, selfishness, greed, and deception get in the way. This includes his relationship with God. Unless God were willing to forgive us (*grace and mercy*), we could have no relationship with Him, for *we are unable to be sinless before Him.* Therefore, if you thought you were sinless before Him, then you are not who you thought you were. I believe the church without a spot or wrinkle is to be; those who realize this, a man who has escaped a snare that had previously entrapped him, know what true freedom feels like and want the others who are still trapped to feel what he is feeling: true freedom from the snares. This is why Jesus taught: to do unto others as you would have them do unto you. Truthfully, you would be very angry if two of you were trapped; one got free and did not try to save you; they just thought about themselves, ran off, and left you behind. When you learn to forgive, this is what it feels like: you feel like you just rescued them from the trap that forgiveness got you out of, and now both of you are free. To experience true forgiveness, you first must learn to forgive; that experience allows you to know exactly what the one you forgive feels. Not forgiving destroys you; it becomes a burden, a heavy weight that you choose to carry around everywhere you go, wearing you down. It is like toting a bag of bricks all the time when all you have to do is set the bag down and walk away; an unnecessary burden. Remember, grace and mercy were extended to you; likewise, you should extend the same to another. If we always put ourselves in the position of the one seeking forgiveness, it becomes a little easier to see the importance of forgiveness because, if you were them, you would want them to forgive you. Awareness is the key to the truth, and the truth will set you free. Because we know what forgiveness feels like, that should be our motive for forgiving another. Where am I going with this? Well, glad you asked. Your close associate or friend, if you choose to call them such, picked you up in their vehicle; the two of you went to a social event; during the time you were together, your associate did something that caused you shame, hurt, and embarrassment; it made you angry to the point of wanting to sever the relationship. Now you realize, you don't know anybody there except your associate, so you're thinking, since this is my ride home, you temporarily forgive them until they get you home, safe and sound. Now, tomorrow you begin; the not speaking to them anymore phase. Forgiveness doesn't work that way; forgiveness is not temporary.

Some believe that because Jesus, in His last seven sayings [*Luke 23:34 KJV*], uttered "Father, forgive them; for they know not what they do" that repentance is not necessary for forgiveness. Well, consider this: Those for whom our Lord then prayed were the soldiers who nailed Him to the cross, to whom the work was but as part of their duty (grace was at work here). However, I could see how thinking of His intercession as including all who, in any measure, sin against God as not knowing what they do, who speak or act against the Son of Man without being guilty of the sin against the Holy Ghost. Consider the prayer was uttered not only for the Roman soldiers, who were mere instruments of the executors, but for all His enemies. The Roman soldiers knew not what they did; they were ignorant at this time that He was the Son of God, and as they were merely obeying the command of their rulers. They know not what they do; it was done through ignorance, *Acts 3:17 KJV*. Paul says, "Had they known it, they would not have crucified the Lord of glory," *1 Corinthians 2:8 KJV*. Ignorance does not excuse a crime altogether if the ignorance is willful, but it diminishes its guilt. Awareness is the key to the truth, and the truth will set your mind free.

17 Chapter

Being a servant
(Do Unto Others)

"Therefore, whatever you want men to do to you, do also to them, for this is the Law and the Prophets", *Matt 7:12, Luke 6:31 KJV*. Restore mentally with the word of God to pre-fall state; let them know you ain't tripp'n because it could have happened to you; bear with them through this process in which it takes for them to reach the state they were before the fall; Remember *Humpty Dumpty*: an egg; a symbol of fertility, creation, but also fragility. The egg holds the life process, the DNA, and the end preexists in the means; Humpty would not have fallen if he had not lifted himself above all others (*pride*). Humpty fell and was shattered into pieces that no man could put back together; our hard shells (*ego*) must be broken for us to let go of who we thought we were so that we can become what we might be; minus the hard shell, only God can take the soft inner workings and make us new, and not necessarily scrambled, but we have to be patient with them that fall until that happens. "Do Good to all, especially to those who are of the household of faith" *Galatians 6:1-2,10 KJV*. We are part of one another, and we are to live for one another in harmony and mutual concern. We are all part of the same Christ.

We often forget this, or it only becomes important when we want someone to treat us as we have treated them well. What about when we treat others badly? Do we want the same? The key is LOVING them as you love yourself. If what you do is out of love, then it shall all be good. Now, you should expect a good return on your investment. *Micah 6:8 KJV* tells us to do justly, love mercy, and walk humbly.

In this life, love appears to be absent; even when we say we love others, we rarely mean "without conditions", nor do we seek their greatest good; not saying to do this is a piece of cake; it takes work and prayer to accomplish. If conditions (*I love you because*) follow love, is it love? *Example:* I love you because you are 36-24-36. What happens when they are no longer 36-24-36? If you no longer love them when that cause changes, can we say you love the body instead of the person? We should be people after God's own heart. Our passion for what God wants should override our intentions and desires; we should seek the greatest good for others. "An individual has not started living until he can rise above the narrow confines of his individualistic concerns to the broader concerns of all humanity", *Martin Luther King Jr.*

When the children of Israel sinned while Moses was upon the mountain, was it the man who instigated the sin or the children who yielded to it? A popular phrase: *'The Devil Made Me Do It*". The wrong that you are accountable for is only the wrong you yielded to. Whatever you are suggested to do by any source, good or evil, yielding is your primary responsibility and accountability; *the end preexists in the means.* If this wrong affects someone who has shown nothing but love for you, and your actions caused them suffering, and you yield to it, that's not showing love to the other person. Flip the situation and see if you want to be the person being wronged by someone you thought loved you. Some of us are afraid to love because it means caring and walking in the light; a burden that is not so easily desired, but we long to be loved. Caring for another means letting go of your dark deeds and walking in the light. "We can easily forgive a child who is afraid of the dark; the real tragedy of life is when men are afraid of the light", *Plato, 1 John 2:8-11.*

"So that you may prove yourselves to be blameless *and* guileless, innocent *and* uncontaminated, children of God without blemish in the midst of a [morally] crooked and [spiritually] perverted generation, among whom you are seen as bright lights [beacons shining out clearly] in the world [of darkness]", *Philippians 2:15 AMP*. How can we share the truth if we are afraid of it (*The Light*)? People who find ways to enhance the law are considered responsible, while people who find ways around it are considered irresponsible. It is easy to harm another without thinking. But, to do good to another, without thinking? No, this requires thought; making such a decision comes from feeding your mind good things. What do you feed your mind? What do you think about often? Paul encourages us in *Philippians 4* to focus on things that are true, honest, just, pure, lovely, and of good report.

Someone once wrote: "All men are made of the same; by the same God. Imagine a stone-faced wall; the large stones will not look so beautiful without the smaller ones keeping them in place. A poor man is as important to God as a King". It shouldn't be about receiving recognition for the good you've done; good is what you should be doing anyway, and that is your responsibility. When you do what is right, someone always notices, and your doing right might cause them to do right without you having to tell them they are doing wrong; it is called paying it forward, leading them into righteousness. Leading by example always works better than leading by instruction.

Being a servant (*Caring for another, seeking their greatest good*) exposes who you are, no costume or disguise. People sometimes like to hide who they are while talking about themselves; they fear they may not be who they thought they were, or who you thought they were. Sometimes it's the Sunday school teacher, the Deacon, and the Pastor, who sometimes wear the mask; they tell you all about themselves while leading you to believe they are talking about others. Sometimes people do what they do during the week, but not things they can share on Sunday morning without the mask. According to *Romans 14*, Christians should exercise personal liberties with caution, for it may destroy another Christian. As discussed in the chapter Cause and Effect, we are a part of each other; what we say and do affects others. We are a part of the body of Christ, which connects us. God does not want us to live in isolation from other believers, so He made it so that we cannot make it alone; this is why we must pray for each other continually. Therefore, we must always be alert as to how our actions affect others. If something we do harms another person, we must take that into account. If what we consider our liberties causes hurt to a brother or sister in Christ, then love should dictate that we limit those liberties around weaker believers. Seeking the greatest good of another is always considering their welfare; happiness, prosperity, etc, understanding their point of view, being respectful to their position or present state, and being committed to the relationship. We are our Brother's keeper. *Psalms 15:1-5* states that we should keep our promise even if it hurts us because this is our responsibility as one who loves another as themselves. Do not charge interest on money you lend, and take money to harm another; only do that which you wish to receive. Do not refuse to care for another because it is a burden; that is why you should do it. Jesus said He will sustain you, so you don't give up on caring and allow satan to cause you to think it is useless. "Cast thy burden upon the LORD, and he shall sustain thee: he shall never suffer the righteous to be moved", *Psalms 55.22 KJV*. Delaying is a form of lacking self-control. Delaying can cause another to stumble, *Romans 13:14 KJV*. "Delay is the deadliest form of denial", *C. Northcote Parkinson.*

Unselfish dedication to the common welfare of others in Christ is our spiritual obligation.

Thus says the Lord: "This is what the Lord says: "Let not the wise boast of their wisdom or the strong boast of their strength or the rich boast of their riches, but let the one who boasts boast about this: that they have the understanding to know me, that I am the Lord, who exercises kindness, justice and righteousness on earth, for in these I delight," declares the Lord" *Jeremiah 9:23-24 NIV*.

Being a servant requires us to exercise gentleness; "Gentleness as a Christian virtue is often closely related to kindness and is the opposite of being intrusive and obnoxious; God is not intrusive nor is He obnoxious; He gave us the choice and the tools we need to do what He asks if we choose to, then He left it at that. "It is exhibited in tenderness, softness, and the conscious exercise of loving caution in dealing with people. It is very concerned about "where other people are at" and seeks to befriend and come alongside to help. It is not cowardly, however, but strong and caring. It shares the truth, listens attentively, and asks permission before blindly speaking into someone's life." *Unknown*. Gentleness is said to be "power under control". Awareness is the key to the truth, and the truth will set your mind free. "The greatest good you can do for another is not to share your own riches, but to reveal to him, his own", *Benjamin Disraeli*.

Chapter 18

Life's Only True Satisfaction
(*What's Love Got To Do With It?*)
Love is life's only true satisfaction. *Proverbs 10:12*

    A parent who loves their children will teach them love at all costs. "Love is our true destiny. We do not find the meaning of life by ourselves alone. We find it with another", *Thomas Merton.*

    Love is seeking the greatest good of another, plain and simple; not to say it is easy to arrive here; it takes a lot of prayer and work; liking them takes even more work. Some view love as an accident; it is more likely for a person to fall accidentally than on purpose, so when using the phrase "fall in love", it sounds like an accident. Love should be a conscious choice. Well, at least unconditional (*AGAPE*) love should be a choice. God chose to love us even before we existed. Some even consider love an emotion, but emotions do not seek another's greatest good. Seeking the greatest good of another means acting in their best interest, always considering their needs, always trying to understand their viewpoint, always treating the other with respect, and being committed to the relationship; this is what God does. Relationships require reciprocation; love cannot be one-way; it has to be both ways. God chose to love us, knowing that we would not reciprocate his love directly. But we should give it our best shot anyway. Yes, God said for us to love Him with all our heart, mind, and soul. This is mentioned in several verses, both the Old and New Testaments; one being *Matthew 22:37*. Jesus also said: A new commandment I give to you in *John 13:34-35,* not to say: stop trying to love God but, *verse 35* states: all men will know we are His by the love we have for each other; this is a way for us to reciprocate His love for us. Unselfish dedication to the common welfare of others is our spiritual obligation, especially to other believers. *Romans 12* gives us a guide to the method of agape love. Keep in mind that love also involves chastening.

A child out of control is usually, but not always, a child who never had principles, precepts, respect, and honor practiced at home. They may have been told these things, but have yet to see this action in the home to learn from these actions. If the parents don't encourage respect out of love, what's the child to do? It is hard to practice what you don't know or haven't been taught. "To the man who only has a hammer, everything he encounters begins to look like a nail", *Abraham Maslow.* A child who knows love will most likely practice love, but a child who knows no love will do the opposite. Often, we get angry with our children for being who they are (*a child without guidance*), when our anger should be directed at the bad parent who failed to teach them because they wanted to spare them the form of discipline they experienced growing up. "He who withholds the rod [of discipline] hates his son, but he who loves him disciplines *and* trains him diligently *and* appropriately [with wisdom and love]", (*Proverbs 13:24AMP*). Do not withhold discipline from the child; if you swat him with a reed-like rod (translated from the Hebrew word *shebet*) [applied with godly wisdom], he will not die. You shall swat him with the reed-like rod and rescue his life from Sheol (the nether world, the place of the dead)", *Proverbs 23:13-14 AMP*. Figurative or physical, however, you choose to receive this passage, the bottom line is that no child should be without correction.

"Spanking should be used when it is clear that misbehavior is deliberate, especially when the child often defies the house rules deliberately. It should be used only when the child receives at least as much praise for good behavior as correction for problem behavior", *Parent magazine*. Also, tell them how proud you are of them when they do things correctly. But, you must also let them know when you disapprove of their behavior, with corrective actions, because you love them that much [*Hebrews 12:6 says* For whom the Lord loveth he chasteneth, and scourgeth every son whom he receiveth]. "Spanking should not occur when a parent is out of control. Parents sometimes need to chill out before administering correction", *Parent magazine*. This is not to promote abuse; there is a difference. Truth: At times, we thought some of our parents may have gone too far and could be considered abuse, but they did it out of love; they sought our greatest good. We were not to be given over to darkness, and they took immediate actions to (*as they saw it*) save us from darkness. "No matter how dark the moment, love and hope are always possible", *George Chakiris*. To see a product of love, growing deeper into love, makes your heart feel good. You feel proud to call them your own. This is what God wants from us. God wants to be proud to show us off as He did, showing satan His confidence in Job (*Job 1:8*). *"It is easier to build strong children than to repair broken men", Frederick Douglass.*

"Being deeply loved by someone gives you strength, while loving someone deeply gives you courage", *Unknown*. Think about this: You may be afraid of certain things, but if facing your fears to protect the ones you love is at hand, you forget the fear the moment you go into protective mode. You will fight twelve men with only a toothpick as a weapon to protect the ones you love. I didn't say you would win, but it can happen; you never know what God is up to; ask David when he faced Goliath *1 Samuel 1.7* The point is that the courage from being loved is your adrenaline, and you will sleep better knowing you weren't hiding in the bushes instead of helping your loved ones who were being attacked.

Our parents are stewards of what God has given them (*Us, you, and me*). They are entrusted with our care and well-being. We must be stewards of what they have given us, their namesake. As Abraham's steward, Eliezer (*Genesis 24*), was so in tune with the way Abraham thought that he was able to make decisions as if he were Abraham himself concerning the affairs that he had to deal with. We have been around our parents long enough to know how not to misrepresent their names. Awareness is the key to the truth, and the truth will set your mind free. "Man must evolve for all human conflict a method which rejects revenge, aggression, and retaliation. The foundation of such a method is love", *Martin Luther King, Jr.*

We must love others also, not just our children. "A new commandment I give unto you, that ye love one another; as I have loved you, that ye also love one another". [Only love can replace revenge, aggression, and retaliation]. "By this shall all men know that ye are my disciples, if ye have love, one to another", *John 13:35 KJV.*

Most of us have, more than once or twice, experienced the act of reproach: *an expression of rebuke or disapproval* of another. The word of God says we should do this in love; if you don't know love, then this will be hard to do; without love, it could get out of hand; blow up into separation; not speaking to one another; dissolve relations, etc. If you love the other and you seek their greatest good, then you should be aware of what sends them into orbit. Never use those methods that cause them to fly off the handle; ask God to show you the way, as He did for Nathan when he told David *2 Samuel 12:1-7, 13,* then you will be using His words and not yours. The Word acts as a reflecting glass; it allows us to see for ourselves how we are. *Perception is not always reality; are you who you thought you were?*

Ruth is a perfect example of seeking the greatest good of another. Ruth lived for the Lord; she was a beacon of light for others. *Read the book of Ruth*

God's love for us is absolute; nothing less than total; He leaves no doubt in our minds as to His commitment to us. He created all the beauty in this world before He created Man; He inspected all that He created and said, "It is good". The Lord goes so far as to establish a covenant with Israel at Mount Sinai and with us at Calvary, as an expression of His absolute commitment to us. We should have two responses: we should love fully the God who first loved us, and, if we are to love our *family* as God loves us, we must not leave doubt in their minds as to the totality of our love for them. Communicate your love to them in certain terms. Some families only know love in a sense, not in its fullness. The parents love their children, but do not teach them how to love.

Therefore, you have parents, loving children, and children who do not love the parents. Respect is the greater part of love, or love causes one to respect another. Parents who fail to teach their child respect result not only in disrespect for them but also for others. They say "what" and "yeah" to their parents and elders instead of "yes, sir" and "yes ma'am", etc. Those who hear saying "yes, sir and yes, ma'am," have a greater respect for their elders because they were raised that way. Honoring parents these days is scarce; the new-age methods of parenting desire to befriend their children, not to parent them; if you can be both, that's okay. But, first, the parent is to guide the children; nowadays, children tell parents what to do. The parents dress like their children, hang out in the same places as their children, listen to the same music as their children; it is hard to tell who is who. If dad is sagging his pants, uses foul language most of the time, wants to fight all the time, and carries a gun under his shirt all the time, then what is the son to do? If mom wears clothes a size too small to show that she still has it going on; acts like a character in a rap song in the presence of her daughter, and allows men to disrespect her in the presence of her daughter, then what is the daughter to do? One or both parent's way of thinking indicates that owning all the famous brands of clothing, electronics, or vehicles, etc., is what should be more important rather than their character. This is not seeking their greatest good; you're ruining them; *the end preexists in the means.*

To seek the greatest good of another, first, we must know who we are and our role in the relationship; if we know what it is about ourselves that we despise, we should steer our loved ones away from that way of thinking. For e*xample*, if you are short-tempered and easily provoked, then you should encourage your loved ones to exercise patience and long-suffering; since that is not your character, find someone who has those traits and let them help mentor you and your children. If you are conceited; and selfish, then you need to encourage selflessness and open-mindedness to others' lack of what they possess; if your loved ones are talented; encourage them not to excess over their talent, but be willing to teach someone else what they know; not looking down on those that are not where they are; since that is not your character, find someone who has those traits and let them help mentor you and your children.

Do not allow your pride to deny you the available help; that's just satan's way of keeping you in darkness. Love dictates that if your child is struggling with a particular subject in school, you seek a tutor to help that child better understand that subject, because this is what Jesus did for us by sending the Holy Spirit after His departure; this is our tutor, He helps us fully understand the things of God. satan, in his subtle ways, is leading you to destruction because his mission is to deceive and destroy the belief in God's way [opposition to divine authority]. If you don't know how to teach your children respect because you were never taught respect, then seek help from someone whose children you have noticed are very respectful to their elders. Seeking their greatest good is not making sure they have the latest pair of famous-brand shoes, but ensuring that you: do all you can to keep their soul from satan. Doing all you can to build strong character in them. Awareness is the key to the truth, and the truth will set you free.

"A family is a place where minds come in contact with one another. If these minds love one another, the home will be as beautiful as a flower garden. But if these minds get out of harmony with one another, it is like a storm that plays havoc with the garden", *Buddha*. There is speculation that this is not a Buddha quote; it is believed to have originated from Japan or elsewhere. The origin is not that important here, but what it says is true.

"Love is patient, love is kind. It does not envy, it does not boast, it is not proud. It does not dishonor others, it is not self-seeking, it is not easily angered, and it keeps no record of wrongs. Love does not delight in evil but rejoices with the truth. It always protects, always trusts, always hopes, and always perseveres. Love never fails. But where there are prophecies, they will cease; where there are tongues, they will be stilled; where there is knowledge, it will pass away". *1Corinthians13:4-8 NIV*. "The only thing necessary for the triumph of evil is for good men to do nothing", *Edmund Burke*. Pray that good men do something. "A friend is someone who knows all about you and still loves you", *Elbert Hubbard*. Pray for a friend like that. "Being deeply loved by someone gives you strength, while loving someone deeply gives you courage", *Unknown*. Pray for love like that.

"I have decided to stick with love. Hate is too great a burden to bear", *Martin Luther King, Jr*. Love means sharing our joys and our pain with the ones we love, and believing that the love between you and them is strong enough to withstand anything.

Voting gives you the power to elect change in your community; to intelligently choose people or things that give you the best chance at bringing the type of change you desire or is needed to improve your community. Well, love is also a choice that gives you the power to elect change in your life and community. Love is a vehicle by which you can move hate to another location; vote it out; change its position of power; give things a new look, and take back your life and community. When satan deceived you into accepting hate as your vehicle of choice, you were viewed as the one who loves to hate. satan used you to tear down the things of God because you were led to hate them; you thought they were depriving you of the joy of life. You were missing the joy of life without love. Awareness is the key to the truth, and the truth will set you free. "Live simply. Love generously. Speak truthfully. Breathe deeply. Do your best. Leave everything else to the powers above you", *Unknown.*

Conclusion

People, having no desire for the truth, are blind. "The truth is not for all men, but only for those who seek it", *Ayn Rand*. We talked about fearing the unknown, which, in most cases, is the truth. Is truth unknown, and is that why we fear it? Those who deny accountability or the responsibility of sharing it (*truth*) with someone else are still responsible due to a large majority of the people choosing to believe a lie rather than the truth, being that a lie is more commonly told, making it easier to; believe; you know, Santa, Easter Bunny, being more excited about Halloween than any of the fore mentioned; to dress up like someone else. For example, all the things children are told that Santa is, God is all those things. Now, when children discover this truth, they also discover that they have been deceived. This is the deception of Santa, I mean satan. He has destroyed their belief system; now you tell them about God; they become skeptics (*Deception*). Perception determines how we believe; if our perception is wrong, we believe in error because perception is not always reality.

Whether the truth is believed or not, or accepted by the majority, does that make it non-truth? We saw this in the days of Noah; the majority did not believe; the rain was coming. Truth is: believing what God said; this is what honors God. We can reject it, we can; throw it out of schools, vote it out of our lives, but it will still be the truth. If we put more energy into practicing love and time executing the results thereof, we might discover that we no longer have time to hate. This also honors God. The funny side is that some would say: "I hate no one, I love everybody", but at the same time, they make a practice of treating people differently because they are not like them or believe as they believe; we should love them but disagree with their differences if it is against God's ways. Remember the story of the Good Samaritan (*Luke 10*)? You either practice love or hate; only the two exist. "Love is greater than faith and hope, making it the central characteristic of Christian Living. All three: Love, Faith, and Hope require a belief in something greater than yourself", *Unknown*.

The truth exposes everything hidden because truth is the light; the light brings about awareness of what is; awareness allows you to see what you were doing in the dark, just as Jacob discovered in *Genesis 29. When the morning came*, he had been deceived. In *Psalms 8:4-6*, David understood that there is a Being capable of creating such perfection and splendor, and must have a great plan and a purpose for us. Well, He does; He wants to reveal that purpose to us, to show us the way out of the pain and the sorrow we have brought on ourselves (*self-inflicted wounds*) from rejecting His ways. He gave the invitation: "Call to Me, and I will answer you, and show you great and mighty things, which you do not know" (*Jeremiah 33:3KJV*). Some things we know are not good for us, yet we choose them anyway; be aware of these things. Your choices determine your results; *the end preexists in the means*. God does not protect us from the consequences of our foolishness. This is the truth. "All truths are easy to understand once you discover them. The point is to discover them," *Galileo*.

To explain in more detail the statement previously made, "The consequence of our own foolishness, God does not protect us from those". If He has a specific task for us as He did for Samson, it is predestined before our existence, then he does protect us from our foolishness to a point, as long as it is not something he specifically told us not to do, like Sampson (*Judges Chapters 13-19*). Wearing house slippers to your favorite shopping place is a perfect example. Now, when your feet go bad, you tell the church to pray for your healing; the pastor is wasting oil on you; asking that God heal your feet that you messed up; you have shoes that you could have worn, but you chose to self-inflict yourself instead; *the end preexists in the means*, that's just what that is. God made it plain in *Galatians 6*: whatsoever you sow, you reap.

"This day I call the heavens and the earth as witnesses against you that I have set before you life and death, blessings and curses. Now choose life, so that you and your children may live" (*Deuteronomy 30:11-19 KJV*).

Love is the cause that effectively affects people, sometimes we go in circles because we can't see the path, it's just because we believe we are smarter than the average bear and we tell ourselves; it is what it is, but this stems from self-inflicted wounds that are often initiated by dictated living; things you didn't see because you were too busy looking. In some cases, vanity might be the reason greed did not reveal the deception, which was at work because we might have been in a state of "hurry up and wait". Selfishness is the syndrome that misleads or deceives [most often]. If we learn to trust in God's plan, we learn to live a life of integrity and develop a giving spirit; we learn to forgive and to be servants. In the end, we learn that love is life's only true satisfaction. Thanks for reading, and may God bless the reader.

Quotes Disclaimer

Quotes Disclaimer for use in this book
All content cited is derived from their respective sources. If you believe we have used your copyrighted content without permission, send an email to dotboy1999@gmail.com.

"Cause and effect, means and ends, seed and fruit, cannot be severed; for the effect already blooms in the cause, the end preexists in the means, the fruit in the seed." *Ralph Waldo Emerson, "Self-Reliance: An Excerpt from Collected Essays, First Series."*

"When I disagree with a rational man, I let reality be our final arbiter; if I am right, he will learn; if I am wrong, I will; one of us will win, but both will profit". *Ayn Rand (2016). "Atlas Shrugged", p.781, Hamilton Books.*

"Reason is not automatic those who deny it cannot be conquered by it. Do not count on them; leave them alone" *Ayn Rand, "Journals of Ayn Rand".*

"Contradictions do not exist. Whenever you think you are facing a contradiction, check your premises. You will find that one of them is wrong." *Ayn Rand "Atlas shrugged"*

"We can evade reality, but we cannot evade the consequences of evading reality" *Ayn Rand "The Objectivist Ethics" 1961.*

"The truth is not for all men, but only for those who seek it" *Ayn Rand. "BrainyQuote.com. Brainy Media Inc,"*

"There's too much tendency to attribute to God the evils that man does of his own free will" *Agatha Christie "The Moving Finger 1942."*

"He who is not contented with what he has, would not be contented with what he would like to have." *Socrates "The Socrates Method".*

"I cannot teach anybody anything. I can only make them think" *Socrates "The Socrates Method".*

"I am the wisest man alive, for I know one thing, and that is that I know nothing." *Socrates, "The Socrates Method."*

"True wisdom comes to each of us when we realize how little we understand about life, ourselves, and the world around us." *Socrates "Thequotesarchive.com"*

"We can easily forgive a child who is afraid of the dark; the real tragedy of life is when men are afraid of the light" *Plato. "The Socrates Method."*

"We are so accustomed to disguise ourselves to others, that in the end, we become disguised to ourselves" *François La Rochefoucauld, "quotes.net, Stands4.LLC."*

"Superman is, after all, an alien life form. He is simply the acceptable face of invading realities" *Clive Barker. "s.gr-assets.com/quotes/78426."*

"I told her I'd wait forever for her, but that was before I found somebody else who'd give me a ride home" *Jarod Kintz "This Book is Not for Sale."*

"Do not wish to be anything but what you are, and try to be that perfectly" *Francis Desales "Goodreads.com"*

"Worse than telling a lie is spending your whole life staying true to a lie", *Robert Brault "Quotes.net. STANDS4 LLC."*

"We must be willing to let go of the life we planned so as to have the life that is waiting for us" *Joseph Campbell. "A Joseph Campbell Companion: Reflections on the Art of Living."*

"It's a hard thing to discover, that what you've always wanted, is of no value to you at all" *Unknown.*

"Better to remain silent and be thought a fool, than to speak out, and remove all doubt", *Abraham Lincoln. "Golden Book 1931."*

"To the man who only has a hammer, everything he encounters begins to look like a nail" *Abraham Maslow. "BrainyQuote.com. Brainy Media Inc,"*

"Love is the only force capable of transforming an enemy into a friend" *Martin Luther King, Jr. "BrainyQuote.com. Brainy Media Inc,"*

"Nothing in the world is more dangerous than sincere ignorance and conscientious stupidity". *Martin Luther King, Jr. "Strength To Love."*

"An individual has not started living until he can rise above the narrow confines of his individualistic concerns to the broader concerns of all humanity". *Martin Luther King, Jr. "BrainyQuote.com. Brainy Media Inc,"*

"I have decided to stick with love. Hate is too great a burden to bear." *Martin Luther King, Jr. "BrainyQuote.com. Brainy Media Inc,"*

"I refuse to accept the view that mankind is so tragically bound to the starless midnight of racism and war that the bright daybreak of peace and brotherhood can never become a reality… I believe that unarmed truth and unconditional love will have the final word." *Martin Luther King, Jr. "BrainyQuote.com. Brainy Media Inc,"*

"Every man must decide whether he will walk in the light of creative altruism or in the darkness of destructive selfishness" *Martin Luther King, Jr." "Strength To love"*

"Human progress is neither automatic nor inevitable. Every step toward the goal of justice requires sacrifice, suffering, and struggle; the tireless exertions and passionate concern of dedicated individuals" *Martin Luther King, Jr. "Goodreads.com"*

"Man must evolve for all human conflict a method which rejects revenge, aggression, and retaliation. The foundation of such a method is love" *Martin Luther King, Jr. "Martin Luther King's Nobel Prize Acceptance Speech 1964"*

"He who controls others may be powerful, but he who has mastered himself is mightier still" *Lao Tzu. "BrainyQuote.com. Brainy Media Inc,"*

"When I let go of what I am, I become what I might be" *Lao Tzu. "BrainyQuote.com. Brainy Media Inc,"*

"If you do not change direction, you might end up where you are heading" *Lao Tzu. "BrainyQuote.com. Brainy Media Inc,"*

"Being deeply loved by someone gives you strength, while loving someone deeply gives you courage" *Unknown. "BrainyQuote.com. Brainy Media Inc,"*

"Most people are other people. Their thoughts are someone else's opinions, their lives a mimicry, their passions a quotation" *Oscar Wilde. "De Profundis"*

"Man is least himself when he talks in his own person. Give him a mask, and he will tell you the truth" *Oscar Wilde. "AZquotes.com"*

"You will never achieve what you are capable of if you're too attached to things you're supposed to let go of" *Unknown.*

"To be yourself in a world that is constantly trying to make you something else is the greatest accomplishment" *Ralph Waldo Emerson. "Brainyquotes.com. Brainy Media Inc,"*

"What was silent in the father speaks in the son, and often I found in the son the unveiled secret of the father." *Friedrich Nietzsche. "AZQuotes.com"*

"Before the effect, one believes in different causes than one does after the effect" *Friedrich Nietzsche. "fnietzsche.com"*

"Vanity well fed is benevolent, vanity hungry is spiteful" *Mason Cooley. "Azquotes.com"*

"And ever has it been known that love knows not its own depth until the hour of separation" *Khalil Gibran "The Coming of the Ship."*

"Doubt is a pain too lonely to know that faith is his twin brother" *Khalil Gibran. "goodnewsnetwork.org"*

"Neither comprehension nor learning can take place in an atmosphere of anxiety" *Rose Kennedy. "BrainyQuote.com. Brainy Media Inc,"*

"Birds sing after a storm; why shouldn't people feel as free to delight in whatever remains to them?" *Rose Kennedy. "BrainyQuote.com. Brainy Media Inc,"*

"Greed is a sin against God, just as all mortal sins, in as much as man condemns things eternal for the sake of temporal things" *Thomas Aquinas. "wisefamousquotes.com"*

"Greed is a bottomless pit which exhausts the person in an endless effort to satisfy the need without ever reaching satisfaction" *Erich Fromm. "BrainyQuote.com. Brainy Media Inc,"*

"Nothing makes us more vulnerable than loneliness, except greed." *Thomas Harris. "The Silence of the Lambs." (Hannibal Lecter)*

"Every great cause begins as a movement, becomes a business, and eventually degenerates into a racket." *Eric Hoffer. "The Temper of Our Time"*

"Knowledge is; knowing a tomato is a fruit. Wisdom is not putting it in a fruit salad." *Miles Kingston. "AZquotes.com"*

"The Bible does not say money is the root of all evil; it says the *love of money* is the root of all kinds of evil. A poor man who, in his heart, worships the idea of being rich is more vulnerable to its evils than a rich man who has a heart to use it all for the Lord" *Criss Jami.*

"The devil has no power ... except in the dark."*Cassandra Clare, "City of Bones".*

"The devil keeps man from good with a thousand machinations spewed from his belly, so that when a person sighs to do good, he pierces him with his shafts; and when he desires to embrace God with his whole heart in love, he subjects him to poisonous tribulations, seeking to pervert good work before God. And when a person seeks the viridity of virtue, the devil tells him that he does not know what he is doing, and he teaches him that he can set his own law for himself."*Hildegard Of Bingen, "Letter to an abbot".*

"We are all acquainted with demons, aren't we? Sometimes they are more subtle than the Devil in person. They are those things that clutch at us, strangle us, force us to obey them. They control us with great delight, and finally they own us. Demons are certainly as much around today as they were in Jesus' day. They are more subtle, perhaps, and so we think we have outgrown them. Because we call them by other names, we have a way of missing them. But there is still a great force surrounding us that tries to push us into what is not of God." *Macrina Wiederkehr, "A Tree Full of Angels".*

"We all know that light travels faster than sound. That's why certain people appear bright until you hear them speak." *Albert Einstein, "Goodreads.com Quotes"*

"The only thing necessary for the triumph of evil is for good men to do nothing." Attributed to *Edmund Burke, but the originator is unknown.*

"What we do for ourselves dies with us. What we do for others and the world remains and is immortal." *Albert Pike, "Morals and Dogma of the Ancient and Accepted Scottish Rite of Freemasonry."*

"Be the change that you wish to see in the world." Attributed to *Mahatma Gandhi, but not verified. "GoodReads.com Quotes"*

"Just because everything is different doesn't mean anything has changed" *Irene Peter, "BrainyQuote.com. BrainyMedia Inc,"*

"Delay is the deadliest form of denial". *C. Northcote Parkinson, "BrainyQuotes.com. Brainy Media Inc, "*

"One of the deep secrets of life is that all that is really worth doing is what we do for others." *Lewis Carroll, "BrainyQuotes.com. Brainy Media Inc,"*

"The more man meditates upon good thoughts, the better will be his world and the world at large." *Confucius, "Goodnewsnetwork.org."*

Are we faithful at something in an attempt to bring God glory and the greatest good to others, ie., loving them by demonstrating long term commitment to them? Or, are we faithful only to what we want and striving after that? *Crosswalk.com*

"In order for the light to shine so brightly, the darkness must be present." *Francis Bacon, "Citatis.com."*

"Adversity is like a strong wind. It tears away from us all but the things that cannot be torn, so that we see ourselves as we really are."*Arthur Golden, "Memoirs of a Geisha."*

"Love is when the other person's happiness is more important than your own" *H. Jackson Brown, Jr."Life's Little Instruction Book."*

"A friend is someone who knows all about you and still loves you" *Elbert Hubbard, "Fixqutes.com."*

"Being deeply loved by someone gives you strength while loving someone deeply gives you courage" *Unknown, "BrainyQuotes.com. Brainy Media Inc,"*

"In each action, we must look beyond the action at our past, present, and future state, and at others whom it affects, and see the relations of all those things. And then we shall be very cautious" *Blaise Pascal, Pensées. "Psychologytoday.com"*

"Through the law of cause and effect, we choose our destiny. Moreover, we are our own prophets for we constantly project our future state by the seeds we plant in the present" *Cheryl Canfield. "Psychologytoday.com"*

"Remember one thing about democracy. We can have anything we want and at the same time, we always end up with exactly what we deserve" *Edward Albee. "Unleashing Intellectual Capital"*

"Behaviorism, also known as behavioral psychology, is a theory of learning based upon the idea that all behaviors are acquired through conditioning. Conditioning occurs through interaction with the environment. Behaviorists believe that our responses to environmental stimuli shape our behaviors. Strict behaviorists believe that any person could potentially be trained to perform any task, regardless of things like genetic background, personality traits, and internal thoughts (*within the limits of their physical capabilities*); all it takes is the right conditioning" *John B. Watson. "Psychology as the Behaviorist Views It."*

"Prejudice is a great time saver; you can form opinions without having to get the facts." *E. B. White. "Quotefancy.com"*

"The key to everything is patience. You get the chicken by hatching the egg, not by smashing it" *Arnold H. Glasow. "Passiton.com"*

"It is easier to build strong children than to repair broken men." *Frederick Douglass "BrainyQuotes.com. Brainy Media Inc,"*

"The soul that is within me no man can degrade" *Frederick Douglass. "GoodReads.com Quotes"*

"Without a struggle, there can be no progress, those who profess to favor freedom, and disapprove agitation, are like people who want crops without plowing up the ground, they want rain without thunder and lightning" *Frederick Douglass. "BrainyQuotes.com. Brainy Media Inc,"*

"Our attitude towards others determines their attitude towards us "*Earl Nightingale "Azquotes.com"*

"Even though you are on the right track; you will get run over if you just sit there" *Will Rogers. "GoodReads.com Quotes"*

"If you don't have integrity, you have nothing. You can't buy it. You can have all the money in the world, but if you are not a moral and ethical person, you really have nothing" *Henry Kravis. "BrainyQuotes.com. Brainy Media Inc,"*

"Well done is better than well said" *Benjamin Franklin BrainyQuotes.com. Brainy Media Inc,"*

"A person whose mind is quiet and satisfied in God is in the pathway to health" *Ellen G. White.*

"Ellen G. White Review and Herald Articles - Book I of IV", p.1794, Lulu Press, Inc"

"Be helpful even if there's no immediate profit in it" *Susan Ward. "AZquotes.com"*

"The most important thing in life is to learn how to give out love and to let it come in" *Morrie Schwartz. Mitch Alborn's "Tuesday with Morrie"*

"The greatest good you can do for another is not to share your own riches, but to reveal to him, his own" *Benjamin Disraeli. "The Socrates Method."*

"No matter how dark the moment, love and hope are always possible" *George Chakiris. "BrainyQuotes.com. Brainy Media Inc,"*

"The greatest deception men suffer is from their own opinions" *Leonardo da Vinci "The Socrates Method."*

"Knowledge of God's Word is a bulwark against deception, temptation, accusation, even persecution" *Edwin Louis Cole. "Azquotes.com"*

"Adults find pleasure in deceiving a child. They consider it necessary, but they also enjoy it. The children very quickly figure it out and then practice deception themselves" *Elias Canetti. "thecitesite.com"*

"Whenever, therefore, people are deceived and form opinions wide of the truth, it is clear that the error has slid into their minds through the medium of certain resemblances to that truth" *Socrates. "The Socrates Method"*

"Vision is not enough; it must be combined with venture. It is not enough to stare up the steps; we must step up the stairs" *Vaclav Havel. "GoodReads.com Quotes"*

"Rivers, ponds, lakes, and streams; they all have different names, but all contain water. Just as religions do, they all contain truths." *Muhammad Ali "BrainyQuotes.com. Brainy Media Inc,"*

"It is wonderful how much time good people spend fighting the devil. If they would only expend; the same amount of energy loving their fellow men, the devil would die in his own tracks of ennui" *Helen Keller. "BrainyQuotes.com. Brainy Media Inc,"*

"However unworthy of honor a father may be, he still retains, since he is a father, his right over his children, provided it does not in anywise derogate from the judgment of God; for it is too absurd to think of absolving under any pretext the sins which are condemned by His Law; nay, it would be a base profanation to misuse the name of father for the covering of sins" *John Calvin "Calvin's Commentary on the Bible, Exodus 20"*

About The Author

Bio

I am Christopher Johnson (*most often Chris*), a first-time author, the youngest of seven children, born and raised in Dallas, Texas. Being the youngest, I became a natural observer of people's behavior. Curiosity has always led me into things, but not all good; I survived. I investigated the perceptions that led me to believe what I thought I was observing, and oftentimes, that perception was not a reality. Learning to ask the right questions awarded me answers that awakened my need to know more about certain behaviors. Some people say what they believe is popular without knowing the true meaning of these things, so I began to compare them with an awareness that led me to a truth (*God's Word*) I could accept. All of the popular sayings were not from God's word, but from even those that don't believe in God, but after comparison, I discovered they said the same thing, just from a different perspective, one that leaves God out because they don't believe. I am a believer in God the Father, Jesus (*The Risen Savior*), God's only begotten son, and the Holy Spirit of God that comforts and guides us to the things of God. I believe in the death, burial, and resurrection of Jesus Christ. I believe that if we change our thinking, we change our lives. Awareness is the key to the truth, and the truth will set you free. I attended Arts Magnet High School in Dallas, Texas, where I studied music. I am a musician by trade, with music being my passion, and writing is becoming a close second. I have been married for twenty-plus years and am a musician at present. My goal in life is to expose as many as I can to Agape Love, seeking the greatest good of another. I want to change the perception of love so that the perspective of love is understood.

Synopsis

God is capable of creating such perfection and splendor and must have a great plan and a purpose for us. Well, He does; He wants to reveal that purpose to us, to show us the way out of the pain, the sorrow we have brought on ourselves (*self-inflicted wounds*) from rejecting His ways. Perception is what determines how we believe; if our perception is wrong, we believe in error because perception is not always reality.

Love is the cause that effectively affects people, sometimes we go in circles because we can't see the path, it's just because we believe we are smarter than the average bear and we tell ourselves; it is what it is, but this stems from self-inflicted wounds that are often initiated by dictated living; things you didn't see because you were too busy looking. In some cases, vanity might be the reason greed did not reveal the deception, which was at work because we might have been in a state of "hurry up and wait". Selfishness is the syndrome that misleads or deceives [most often]. If we learn to trust in God's plan, we learn to live a life of integrity and develop a giving spirit; we learn to forgive and to be servants. In the end, we learn that love is life's only true satisfaction.

www.ingramcontent.com/pod-product-compliance
Lightning Source LLC
LaVergne TN
LVHW010333070526
838199LV00065B/5731